Inside the
BROKEN
Heart

Inside the BROKEN Heart

GRIEF UNDERSTANDING *for* WIDOWS AND WIDOWERS

JULIE YARBROUGH

Abingdon Press
Nashville

Inside the Broken Heart
Grief Understanding for Widows and Widowers

Cataloging-in-Publication Data has been requested with the Library of Congress.

ISBN 978-1-4267-4444-0

12 13 14 15 16 17 18 19 20 21—10 9 8 7 6 5 4 3 2 1

MANUFACTURED IN THE UNITED STATES OF AMERICA

To my beloved husband, Leighton, now and forever
My life, my joy, my all

Acknowledgments

I am grateful to my grief mentor, the Reverend Patsy Brundige, for her untiring support and inspiration; Susan M. Creagan, M.D. for the gift of her time and humanity; Joyzelle McCreary, PhD. for listening to the layers; Susan for reading and editing; the Reverend Barbara Marcum for her encouragement to share; and the Reverend Bill Smith, who is always there, always. My heart is forever blessed by each person who came and shared their individual experience with the Grief Understanding group at Highland Park United Methodist Church. You saved my life. We cared for each other inside the broken heart.

Contents

Contents

Introduction

We grieve because we love. This book was written to help widows and widowers understand grief in the emotional and physical aftermath of death and to guide the way back to fullness of life. Forever changed, we emerge from the darkness of grief in search of light, the light of new life. "And after you have suffered for a little while, the God of all grace...will himself restore, support, strengthen and establish you" (1 Peter 5:10-11 NRSV).

If you have been on the journey of grief longer than a few days or weeks, perhaps for months or years, likely you have passed the nadir of the valley of the shadow of death. You have been through the darkest hours of anger, fear, and loneliness and are moving gradually, imperceptibly away from death toward life. Life as it is without your husband or wife, life here and now, life as it is becoming.

We all have a story. "We spend our years as a tale that is told" (Psalm 90:9 KJV). My husband, Dr. Leighton Farrell, was Senior Minister of Highland Park United Methodist Church in Dallas, Texas for twenty-three years. In 2004 Leighton was diagnosed with pancreatic cancer and died ninety days later. I was destroyed: my heart shattered into one million small pieces. At fifty-five I was young and very old. I was alone.

Death and grief enjoy a remarkable taboo in our society. Not because of their sacred and inviolable nature, rather because of our innate aversion to the consideration of our own mortality. Like you, I have faced death in the first person. Although I am not a therapist or professional, I have immersed myself in grief literature since the death of my husband, intent on fully understanding my life-altering encounter with grief. Even as I cherish our marriage, the best part of my life, I work to transform the experience of grief into a new life that honors the memory of my beloved husband, a life lived in gratitude for the faithfulness of God.

Death has redemptive value as loss and survival inspire us to greater compassion for the suffering of others. To those whose grief is newer than ours we offer the humanity and wisdom of a life tried and tested. May the promises of the Bible used as topical reference sustain and encourage you to trust in life and contemplate hope inside the broken heart. You are not alone.

Julie Yarbrough
Dallas, Texas

PART I

Inside the Broken Heart

What Is Grief?

Now is your time of grief, but I will see you again and you will rejoice, and no one will take away your joy.

—John 16:22 NIV

The death of our husband or wife is like the death of a part of our self. Grief is the outpouring of emotion and pain that expresses how we feel because of what has happened in our life:

- Grief is shock at the suddenness with which life's plans have been changed.
- Grief is anger at the untimely death of a loved one.
- Grief is sadness.
- Grief is the pain of starting to speak to someone who is no longer there.
- Grief is loneliness.
- Grief is wishing that things were as they used to be and knowing that they never will be again.
- Grief is contemplation as we meditate on the finality of our own earthly life.

We grieve because of a loss we would never desire:

- We did not plan for our husband or wife to die.
- We could not control death—the when, where, how, or why.
- We are powerless to change what has happened.

Though universal in its fundamental attributes, grief is individual and personal. Everyone grieves differently. The idea that it is possible to take charge of one's grief belies the very nature of pain and heartache. No amount of resolve or discipline can determine the course of grief. In *Much Ado About Nothing* William Shakespeare wrote, "Every one can master a grief but he that has it."[1] The head cannot lead; it must follow the heart.

A beloved husband or wife dies, departing our physical, earthly life together. At first we deny grief, mercifully shrouded by shock, fatigue, and numbness. In the emotionally arduous hours and days that follow, we function, still stunned by the bitter reality of death. We experience rites and rituals with vague detachment from a surreal moment in time and space. When the last guest has left, we are alone. Grief assaults us like a tsunami. We are engulfed by uncontrollable weeping, perhaps many times each day. Grief is raw and gut-wrenching, a state of soulless heartache with painful physical symptoms that mirror our emotional devastation.

Grief has a life of its own; it is a restless shadow in the soul, for a while insistent and unavoidable. The dimensions of grief shift from day to day as we contend with the reality of life without our wife or husband. How we incorporate grief into our life is the challenge of each new day. Our lives are shaped by how we deal with the unalterable circumstance of death. Grief never leaves us where it finds us. It leaves us disillusioned or more profound, fearful or more confident in the faithfulness of God, depending on how intently we listen to what grief has to say to us.

In the Christian faith, grief is sometimes framed in self-denial. Many grieving Christians feel guilty for crying or being sad, their rationale being that a person of strong faith should feel happy to know that his or her spouse is in heaven. But grief is not a crisis of faith, it is a crisis of the heart. We can believe beyond doubt that our husband or wife is with God, but we are human. We are in pain. We hurt. This does not mean that we are bad Christians or that our faith is weak. Rather, grieving is really a show of faith. We trust God to hold us at our most vulnerable, when our life is in pieces and our strength is gone. "The eternal God is your refuge, and underneath are the everlasting arms" (Deuteronomy 33:27 NIV). God is with us as we grieve. God shares our tears and sadness. God feels our pain and sorrow. God is with us as we struggle in our brokenness. God promises that grief and pain will not last forever, that we will be restored and made whole again. "Now is your time of grief, but I will see you again and you will rejoice, and no one will take away your joy" (John 16:22 NIV).

Death is nothing at all. I have only slipped away into the next room. I am I, and you are you. Whatever we were to each other, that we are still. Call me by my old familiar name, speak to me in the easy way, which you always used to. Put no difference in your tone; wear no forced air of solemnity or sorrow. Laugh as we always laughed at the little jokes we enjoyed together. Life means all that it ever meant. It is the same as it ever was; there is unbroken continuity.

—Henry Scott Holland (1847–1918), Canon of St. Paul's Cathedral[2]

The Journey

⁓

Even though I walk through the valley of the shadow of death, I fear no evil, for thou art with me.

—*Psalm 23:4 RSV*

In this familiar, beloved scripture, the image is that of the shepherd guiding his sheep through many terrains and perils to reach hillside grazing and safety. The psalmist writes, "Even though I walk through the valley of the shadow of death;" he uses the first person, "I." We know that the one who dies goes through that symbolic valley toward the finality of death, yet we as survivors actually go *through* the valley of the shadow of death. We encounter this place of powerful metaphor as we descend the depths to meet our wounded soul at its most vulnerable. We scale the exigencies of loss and adjustment and slowly make our way to the other side. At last we make our way through grief, our personal valley of the shadow of death.

The experience of grief is often referred to as a journey. A journey is usually longer, more difficult than a short trip. Grief is personal, a first-person journey. One lonely Saturday afternoon a few months after Leighton died, I sat in a movie theater and was struck by advertising for a well-known brand of luggage. As travel images flashed on the screen, the message unfolded that a journey is not a trip or a vacation. Rather, a journey is both a process and a discovery. As a process of self-discovery, a journey brings us face to face with ourselves. On a journey we not only see the world, but we also better understand how we fit into the world. Although I did not rush out and buy the luggage being advertised, the final teaser was powerful. The question was posed whether the person creates the journey or the journey creates the person. In less than sixty seconds the message was clear: "The journey is life itself. Where will life take you?"

When does the journey begin? It starts when grief begins, whether on the actual death date of your husband or wife, or at some time during a period of illness or physical decline. My journey began when Leighton got sick, suddenly and unexpectedly. From the outset life went steadily downhill, steeply declining into the abyss of disbelief and desperation. He died after an illness of only ninety days, our earthly life together abruptly at an end. He left the valley of the shadow of death as I ventured alone, an emotional stranger, into the unknown dark chasm of grief.

Have you ever set out on a trip without some idea of where you were going, the best way to get there, or when you would arrive? We do not know the destination of our grief journey. The unknown path of our journey through the valley of the shadow of death is that which makes grief so arduous. Unexpected setbacks are detours. Unplanned side trips occur with illness or disability. Emotional ups and downs keep us on the uneven pavement of a bumpy road. Interactions with those who do not understand our grief isolate us on the rough shoulders of a narrow, less-traveled highway. The murky road looms ahead with no end in sight. Its large, garish billboards shout, "What is my destination?" "When will I be there?" "How will I know when I am there?"

Consider the analogy of car and driver. From the moment of death, grief is in the driver's seat of our life, a silent, steady companion in charge of the journey until its end. Like a cab or bus ride, we entrust our safety and our life to a driver personally unknown to us. Perhaps you rode in a limousine to the funeral or graveside service for your husband or wife, a means of transportation more a necessity than a luxury at the time, grateful that you did not have to drive yourself. A limousine ride can be pleasurable, but if there is only one passenger with no else along for the ride, there is nothing and no one to hold onto. Every turn feels like a boat careening around a sharp corner. The lone passenger is tossed about in random motion, like the spin of a carnival ride or the thump and bump of a clothes dryer. This is the journey of grief—solitary and chaotic. We have no control over the route; there is an unfamiliar force in control of our life until we arrive at our destination.

Reluctantly we become acquainted as grief drives on. We engage in conversation; we want to know more about this driver in charge of our life. Somewhere along the way we downsize to a luxury sedan, more stable and comfortable than a limousine. As we progress still further along the journey through grief, we pull over and want to drive ourselves again. We switch to our accustomed vehicle, smaller than a limousine or luxury sedan, more proportionate to our life as it scales to more manageable dimensions. We order grief into the back seat, knowing that it will be with us yet for a while, until someone else needs a capable driver, someone whose grief is newer than ours. Car and driver, our life on the journey through grief.

How do we traverse the valley of the shadow of death? "Even though I walk..." We are not asked to jog, run, or race. We walk. Our journey through grief, through the valley of the shadow of death is slow, laborious foot work, one foot in front of the other, perhaps often only one half-step at a time. We lose our balance, we miss a step, our footing slips, we fall down. We recover our toehold and again inch forward, gaining ground after each setback. We attempt great bounding strides to deal with grief as quickly and expeditiously as possible, but grief will not be hurried or circumvented, there is no easy detour around it. The slow, steady pace of a rhythmic walk will ultimately see us through to the other side. Along the way we acquire the courage, strength, and self-nurture necessary for life after loss.

You may be new to the emotional time travel of grief, reliving every footstep of the journey, counting the days and weeks. You may have been on the road for months, perhaps even years, weary from the endless road ahead. Where we are now illuminates the past and intimates the future. Perspective is the compass that points the way. Time reframes what happened into how we live forward, time allows us to reflect with more than a rear view mirror. "Does the person create the journey, or does the journey create the person?"

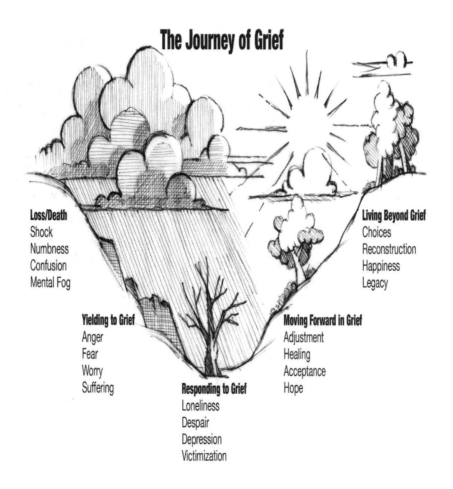

The Journey of Grief

Loss/Death
Shock
Numbness
Confusion
Mental Fog

Yielding to Grief
Anger
Fear
Worry
Suffering

Responding to Grief
Loneliness
Despair
Depression
Victimization

Moving Forward in Grief
Adjustment
Healing
Acceptance
Hope

Living Beyond Grief
Choices
Reconstruction
Happiness
Legacy

"The Journey of Grief" is a road map of the valley of the shadow of death that suggests where we are along the way. A recently widowed acquaintance started a conversation by confessing her depression. She said that until her husband died, they never had any real problems. As she expressed a range of grief emotions, she described her own journey of grief. In the illustration, the words used to describe the topography are personal and expansive; they accurately characterize our grief. Think about the topography of your grief journey. Can you identify personal progress through the valley of the shadow of death?

- Where have you been?
- Where are you now?
- What are the obstacles along the way?
- If you have been on the journey for a while, are you moving forward?
- Where are the oases for quiet and rest?
- Where is your place of "still waters"—a glassy lake, a seaside retreat, a reflecting pool, a burbling fountain?
- What are the signposts along your journey?
- What is your destination?

Each person has a different topography, a unique landscape of grief because of the starting point:

- Did you jump off a cliff into the valley of the shadow of death because of the sudden illness or death of your husband or wife?
- Were you overwhelmed by a landslide of illness that went nowhere but down?
- Were you a caretaker or caregiver for several years before death, your map one of persistent erosion?

᭍ Was the death of your husband or wife like the slow, steady white-hot flow of lava down a mountainside?

The geography of grief includes places and settings that will never again be the same without our husband or wife. If we move from our family home, the physical place of daily life changes, we no longer inhabit the space in which a life together was created and nurtured. We may be unable to enjoy a favorite restaurant or travel destination shared with our husband or wife. We may avoid an accustomed church pew or place that evokes powerful emotion or memory. Along the way, our head and heart signal our direction—where to go, what to avoid. Our head says, "go," our heart says, "broken–stop–don't go." As the geography of grief changes topography from deep valley to expansive plain, it may be less painful, perhaps even pleasurable to revisit places once abandoned in grief.

As we grieve, we create a personal map that charts where we are going in life without our husband or wife. Our map may be like that of Christopher Columbus and his contemporaries. Unable to imagine life beyond the visible horizon, distant shores, or life in undiscovered places, early explorers expected to fall off the edge of the earth. Yet the allure of what might lie beyond inspired them to risk everything for an unknown adventure. They embarked into the future with faith that God would be there to lead them, light the way, and direct their path.

God charts the map of our grief journey through the valley of the shadow of death; he faithfully leads us beside still waters and restores our soul. God's divine destination for us at the end of the journey is peace. Peace does not overwhelm us all at once and for all time. We are not suddenly there. Peace comes in small, elusive moments, fleeting glints of emotional sunshine that warm then fade, moments that recur with greater frequency until our life is more about contentment than pain, less about grief than peace,

peace because we have forgiven ourselves our human insufficiency to death.

peace because we no longer strain against that which we cannot change.

peace because we have traversed the valley of the shadow of death and survived the journey through grief.

You know that you are near the end of the journey when you claim for yourself the gift of peace.

My Lord God, I have no idea where I am going. I do not see the road ahead of me. I cannot know for certain where it will end. Nor do I really know myself, and the fact that I think I am following your will does not mean that I am actually doing so. But I believe that the desire to please you does in fact please you. And I hope I have that desire in all that I am doing. I hope that I will never do anything apart from that desire. And I know that if I do this you will lead me by the right road, though I may know nothing about it. Therefore I will trust you always though I may seem to be lost and in the shadow of death. I will not fear, for you are ever with me, and you will never leave me to face my perils alone.

—Thomas Merton[3]

Anger

Peace I leave with you. My peace I give to you; not as the world gives do I give to you. Let not your heart be troubled, neither let it be afraid.

—*John 14:27 NKJV*

Anger is frequently expressed by men and women who are grieving as an emotional reflex to separation by death from husband or wife. Anger is socially toxic, an emotion we are expected to repress, ignore, and resolve, especially when we grieve. As the inability to control negative emotions, anger is construed as a sign of weakness. Because society has little tolerance for the weak, we assimilate ourselves to a life absent of anger. When we grieve, we are not prepared for the full frontal assault of anger when it shows up unannounced. It may surprise us with its force and power. Anger thrives and consumes vital energy if we provide a place in our heart for it to take root and grow. Eighteenth-century English poet Alexander Pope wrote, "To be angry is to revenge the fault of others upon ourselves."[4]

Although feelings of resentment and anger are normal in grief, it is important to identify the reasons:

- Our husband or wife died.
- We feel abandoned.
- We feel alone.
- We feel the pressure of new responsibilities.

The target of our anger may be:

- husband or wife
- doctors/medical personnel
- family
- well-intentioned friends
- ourselves
- God

It is hard work to sort through the emotions that engulf us after death, simultaneously reconciling ourselves to the loss of husband or wife. As we confront anger, we realize that it is not wrong to experience it as long as we understand its cause. When anger occupies our thoughts, it easily instructs our guilt and regrets.

No survivor is immune to some regret or guilt, whether imagined or real. Regret about words said that should not have been said, or words simply left unsaid. We might have talked more about the disease, or had a "moment of truth" conversation. We might have confessed our fear of death. Our husband or wife might have expressed more concern for our future. We might have said a real good-bye. We might have given or received forgiveness. We might have given or received a last kiss. As we identify unresolved issues of guilt and regret, the space in our heart for the emotional legacy of our husband or wife is cleansed and again made whole.

GUILT AND REGRETS

I should have   I might have   If only I had

In his book *When Bad Things Happen to Good People*, Harold Kushner observes that even the most devoted caregiver may experience that moment when fatigue and fear assume the guise of impatience and anger as exhaustion gives way to exasperation.[5] Leighton was sick unto death. I thought that if he would try, he could get better and rejoin our life. My encouragement had absolutely no effect on his body or spirit. Frustrated by my human impotence, I was angry in my most private heart because I was powerless, unsettling emotional territory for one usually so calm and level. Life as it had been slipped away faster than I could hold on to it. Months passed before I could forgive myself for not being able to save him. When we forgive ourselves, we move forward, commending our experience to the perspective of the past, enlarged to include our humanness.

When we name our anger, we discern who or what it is we need to forgive. As we forgive, we quiet trouble in our heart; we receive peace. "Peace I leave with you, My peace I give to you: not as the world gives do I give to you. Let not your heart be troubled, neither let it be afraid" (John 14:27 NKJV).

> What purpose does my anger serve?
> How long do I want to invest in anger?
> What is my anger covering up?
> How do I resolve my anger?
> • Forgive
>   ~ forgive ourselves
>   ~ forgive others

• Abandon

    ~ allow anger to abate over time

    ~ consciously let go of anger

1. What are the personal issues of grief that make you angry?
2. Are you comfortable with your anger?
3. Is anger a worthy emotional companion on your grief journey?
4. What are you doing to identify and resolve your anger?

Fear

Fear not, for I am with you, be not dismayed, for I am your God; I will strengthen you, I will help you, I will uphold you with my victorious right hand.

—Isaiah 41:10 RSV

For I, the LORD your God, hold your right hand; it is I who say to you, "Fear not, I will help you."

—Isaiah 41:13 RSV

In his book *A Grief Observed*, C. S. Lewis wrote, "No one ever told me that grief felt so like fear."[6] In grief we greet fear every day; for some it seems like every minute of every day. Fear is a normal part of the grieving process.

Fear is "a feeling of agitation and anxiety; a feeling of disquiet or apprehension."[7] Grief magnifies our human capacity for fear. What we most fear becomes reality when our husband or wife dies. Our pursuant agitation, anxiety, and apprehension are the fear of grief. Though fear is a common response to death, it need not permanently define our life.

Eighteenth-century philosopher, orator, and politician Edmund Burke wrote, "No passion so effectually robs the mind of all its powers of acting and reasoning as fear."[8] Fear ambushes us when we are unprepared and least able to defend ourselves. When we grieve, fear threatens to paralyze us. Fear has the power to make us feel incompetent and hopeless. Confidence becomes self-doubt; certainty becomes second-guessing. For a while our strength and wisdom are reduced to weakness. Our world is shaken; we are wounded and broken. In the aftermath of our rude encounter with death we ask in quiet panic, "Who is going to take care of me now that my spouse has died?" We are vulnerable to the kaleidoscopic emotions engendered by fear:

- fear of illness and death
- fear of change
- fear of the unknown
- fear of the future

Other fears are more personal:

- fear of not having enough money
- fear of driving
- fear of living alone
- fear of going to public places
- fear of loneliness
- fear of getting hurt
- fear of dying alone

Journaling can be an invaluable discipline, a retreat unto ourselves while doing the arduous, daily, lonely work of grief. Unexpected words may pour forth that show us where we have been and light the way ahead.

When we write about fear we face it.

- We put it in perspective.
- We consign it to a safe, private place.
- We assess whether it is real.
- We recognize it as the temporary by-product of our life in constant change.

When we do that which we fear,

- We turn it into courage.
- We disable its power.
- We defeat it.
- We become stronger.

As fear dissipates, slowly we regain our emotional equilibrium and self-confidence as we move forward in grief.

> *God is our refuge and strength,*
> *a very present help in trouble.*
> *Therefore we will not fear, though the earth should change,*
> *though the mountains shake in the heart of the sea;*
> *though its waters roar and foam,*
> *though the mountains tremble with its tumult.*
> —Psalm 46:1-3 RSV

1. What is it that I fear?
2. What do I fear will happen?
3. What is the worst that will happen?
4. What will more likely happen?
5. What can I do to disable and conquer my fear?

Worry

Therefore do not worry about tomorrow, for tomorrow will worry about itself. Each day has enough trouble of its own.

—Matthew 6:34 NIV

When we marry, we accept another person into our life as husband or wife and thereby form a partnership of mind, body, heart, and spirit. An emotional trauma of grief is the loss of partnership. The marriage of two is reduced to one, a lifetime partnership involuntarily dissolved by death. Alone we bear the entire load; we manage, cope, and persevere.

In grief our most faithful companion is worry. Concern, anxiety, and worry are often used interchangeably to express emotional distress. Concern easily escalates to worry as we assume sole responsibility for our life. Worry is a learned habit, an acquired state of mind and thought. Some people worry habitually; others are less predisposed to chronic worry. The emotional pain and heartache of grief intensify worry. Our fears drive and inspire worry. When we grieve, worry is a natural reaction to questions we ask every day, "What should I do about...?" "What will I do...?"

~~& What do we worry about, especially when we grieve?
- health
    - ~ What will happen if I get sick?
    - ~ Who will be there to take care of me if I get sick?
    - ~ Where will I live if I get sick?
- the future
    - ~ What is life without my husband or wife?
    - ~ Will I ever be loved again?
    - ~ Will my children be there to love and support me as I age?
- financial security
    - ~ Will I have enough money to live?
    - ~ Who can I trust with my money?
    - ~ Will I have a job and be able to work?

What are you worrying about now?

Anxiety is an expression of fear. It is worry born of grief-driven uncertainty and self-doubt. After the death of a husband or wife, anxiety may cause unaccustomed distress or panic. Anxiety is a visceral reaction to our fear of the unknown, projections about that which may or may not come to pass. Anxiety is characterized by questions such as, "What will happen if . . . ?" "What would happen if . . . ?"

What are you anxious about now?

Agonizing is the most extreme form of worry. It is the non-productive response to our circular inner monologue, the endless conversation of the mind that asks, "What if . . . ?" We agonize subconsciously when we anguish over:

- difficult decisions
- seemingly hopeless situations
- long-term possibilities
- unknown outcomes

What are you agonizing about now?

Worry is a side effect of grief, not a permanent condition. As life becomes more manageable, less driven by fear and insecurity, we conquer worry and defeat anxiety. We are assured that God is larger than our worry, "Therefore do not worry about tomorrow, for tomorrow will worry about itself. Each day has enough trouble of its own" (Matthew 6:34 NIV).

Loneliness

———

And after you have suffered for a little while, the God of all grace, who has called you to his eternal glory in Christ, will himself restore, support, strengthen and establish you.

—1 Peter 5:10-11 NRSV

Loneliness is the overarching experience of grief. It is the pervasive condition of the heart that spans the duration of grief. We commit to a lifetime together with our husband or wife, yet we experience the marriage vow moment, "until death do us part," and find ourselves alone. For a while, loneliness is the steady, ice-cold companion of grief.

Part of the loneliness of grief is the urgent desire to keep our husband or wife alive in our heart and memory. We need to talk, to invoke his or her name, to hear others speak with passion about the life and continuing spiritual presence of our husband or wife. But who is listening, really listening? Who understands our pain and bewilderment? We long to express our grief, to talk about our emotional isolation and loneliness.

Friends and family members who have not experienced the loss of a spouse may be unaware of our need for nurture and understanding. We rationalize and forgive unintentional slights that hurt and confound us. Admonitions to be "done with grief" painfully recall the comfortless, infuriating funeral euphemisms, "he's in a better place," or, "what a blessing." Who is blessed when someone dies? What is the blessing of death except the end of mortal pain and suffering? Words intended to comfort the broken heart overlay grief's pain and deny our loss.

One of the most challenging aspects of grief is eating alone. The empty chair at the kitchen table is always a frustrating encounter with the inescapable, pervasive loneliness of life without our husband or wife. Meals together with our spouse were daily communion, a celebration of life and each other. We shared conversation, ideas, plans, and dreams. The fact is that we must eat to nourish our body. This is the way God created us. Yet in grief we easily become indifferent to our own care and self-nurture. The neglect of proper diet and nutrition is a common manifestation of loneliness. We are forced to reconfigure this part of life, adapting new habits that honor the gift of physical health and well-being.

Our loneliness is in sharp contrast to life going on around us. Until the death of our husband or wife, we were among the carefree, happy people holding hands, laughing, in emotional communion with a beloved partner. We at once isolate and insulate ourselves because we are alone. We relieve isolation and loneliness when we reach out to others:

- Find someone with whom you may speak freely about your husband or wife, ideally another widow or widower. Expressing your emotions will make you feel better.
- Find a spiritual, social, or community support group for widows and widowers. Share with others who understand that loneliness is part of grief.
- Find an objective listener who will offer professional perspective on your personal issues of grief.

❧ "Pray that your loneliness may spur you into finding something to live for, great enough to die for."[9]

In March, 2004 Leighton went to visit a close personal friend who had terminal lung cancer. He loved him and was sad that his friend would soon die. Leighton cherished this final visit, touched by Dick's faith and unfailing good spirit.

Three weeks after Leighton died I read the obituary notice for Dick. It was unimaginable to me that Leighton had become ill and died before his friend. Urged by my own grief to greater compassion for the heartache of another, I wrote a note to Dick's wife, whom I had met only once. Several days later, she called. I did not know her, yet she became my grief friend. We felt safe and comfortable talking with each other. We understood each other's pain and sorrow. We listened and helped each other. I found a friend, a new friend who was on the same journey through grief. We still talk occasionally, less often than at first. We grieve, we remember, we live.

The Stages of Grief

After Nathan had gone home, The LORD struck the child that Uriah's wife had borne to David, and he became ill. David pleaded with God for the child. He fasted and went into his house and spent nights lying on the ground. The elders of his household stood beside him to get him up from the ground, but he refused, and he would not eat any food with them. On the seventh day the child died. David's servants were afraid to tell him that the child was dead, for they thought, "While the child was still living, we spoke to David but he would not listen to us. How can we tell him the child is dead? He may do something desperate." David noticed that his servants were whispering among themselves and he realized the child was dead. "Is the child dead?" he asked. "Yes," they replied, "he is dead." Then David got up from the ground. After he had washed, put on lotions and changed his clothes, he went into the house of the LORD and worshiped. Then he went to his own house, and at his request they served him food, and he ate. His servants asked him, "Why are you acting this way? While the child was alive, you fasted and wept, but now that the child is dead, you get up and eat!" He answered, "While the child was still alive, I fasted and *wept. I thought, 'Who knows? The LORD may be gracious to me and let the child live.' But now that he is dead, why should I fast? Can I bring him back again? I will go to him, but he will not return to me."*

—*2 Samuel 12:15-23 NIV*

In her book *On Death and Dying*, Dr. Elisabeth Kübler-Ross identifies five stages of emotional and psychological response that most people experience when faced with a life-threatening illness or life-changing event: denial and isolation, anger, bargaining, depression, acceptance.[10] It is important to note that Kübler-Ross originally studied these stages *only in people suffering from terminal illness*. Later they were applied to any form of catastrophic personal loss.

The Kübler-Ross stages best describe the clinical structure of dying, death, and grief in the abstract. Understanding the stages may help in the diagnosis of grief. But when we grieve, we do not live in a constant state of clinical self-awareness. Seldom are we consciously aware that we are in a particular stage of our emotional response to death.

As we experience grief, we reference where we are and how we feel rather than the clinical structure of grief suggested by stages. When we grieve, few of us have the mental focus to self-diagnose. For example, seldom do we remark to ourselves, "I am in the stage of denial and isolation." Instead, when we are in this stage, we simply feel shock—indeed, we are often immobilized by shock. At each moment we do not name a stage of grief; rather, we struggle through it with only the will to survive. For this reason, we will explore the spiritual and emotional issues of grief without persistent reference to stages.

To best illustrate the stages of grief, the biblical narrative describes the incipient grief of David, an acclaimed warrior, a musician, and the poet of many psalms. A man of strength, David lived in conflict with himself, torn between ambition, lust, and his desire to serve God, very much like our own contemporary dilemma. The actions of David at the death of his beloved son model our struggle through the stages of grief. Like David, we act and react. We personalize the structure of our experience as we move toward the resolution of our grief.

Our personal reaction to the experience of illness and death is an integral part of the grief journey. If your husband or wife endured the debilitation of illness, you suffered alongside in *denial and isolation*. Frustrated by your own helplessness, you were unable to save your beloved—not so much *from* death, rather *for* life, your life together. *Denial* at first protects us from the incomprehensible: all the force of our human will could not alter the event of death. As reality slowly replaces *denial*, we begin to forgive ourselves our powerlessness over death. Slowly we release our lingering self-recrimination. When we are able to abandon our imagined failure, we are better able to comprehend the reason for our seemingly irrational behavior when we are in *denial* over death.

"After Nathan had gone home, the LORD struck the child that Uriah's wife had borne to David, and he became ill" (2 Samuel 12:15 NIV). We are forced to ask ourselves what we believe. Do we believe that God strikes us down? Do we believe that God causes us to become ill? Do we believe that God determines whether we live or die? Or do we trust in God's plan for life set in motion by mysteries that God alone comprehends? When we have no answers to the mysteries of life and death, we may react in *anger*.

"David pleaded with God for the child. He fasted and went into his house and spent the nights lying on the ground" (2 Samuel 12:16 NIV). David did as we do, especially when calamity strikes our lives. He pled with God; he was *bargaining* for the life of his child. When faced with the reality of illness and death, did we plead with God to spare the life of our husband or wife? Like David, do we bargain with God? As part of our bargaining, have we performed sacrificial acts as an offering to God?

"The elders of his household stood beside him to get him up from the ground, but he refused, and he would not eat any food with them" (2 Samuel 12:17 NIV). Focused only on the vigil at the bedside of our husband or wife, did we ignore the urging of others to eat and sleep? Have we denied ourselves care and sustenance as self-punishment for our imagined failures?

"On the seventh day the child died. David's servants were afraid to tell him that the child was dead, for they thought, 'While the child was still living, we spoke to David, but he would not listen to us. How can we tell him the child is dead? He may do something desperate'" (2 Samuel 12:18 NIV). The fear and dread expressed by the servants may sound like a doctor, nurse, hospice worker, or family member who was reluctant to be the herald of bad news. Were others protecting you from death, afraid to tell you the truth, fearful of your reaction? Were you in denial about imminent death?

"David noticed that his servants were whispering among themselves and he realized the child was dead. 'Is the child dead?' he asked. 'Yes,' they replied, 'he is dead'" (2 Samuel 12:19 NIV). David was not spared harsh reality. No one relied on the euphemisms of death—"he passed away," "he's gone," "he's not with us anymore," to communicate the truth to David. We are affected by the words used to express the fact of death. "He is dead." "She is dead." Often these words signal the onset of grief and *depression*.

"Then David got up from the ground. After he had washed, put on lotions, and changed his clothes, he went into the house of the LORD and worshiped. Then he went to his own house, and at his request they served him food, and he ate" (2 Samuel 12:20 NIV). After David was told that the child was dead, he took action. He got up from the ground. Likely it was cold, hard, and dirty; perhaps it was like the uncomfortable sofa or hospital recliner that was perhaps your resting place for days or weeks.

After the death of your spouse did the first shower or bath seem ritualistic, or normal and cleansing? Did a steady stream of running water allow you to escape from the reality of death for even ten minutes? David then nurtured himself with lotion and a change of clothes. He took time to take care of himself. He took the first step to prepare for the rest of his life, a life without his beloved child.

Finally, he demonstrated his spiritual strength. He went into the house of the Lord and worshiped. We practice our faith at funeral and memorial services, yet often we are incapable of true worship at the time, overwhelmed by the unfamiliar emotions of grief. Because we are in shock, worship seems almost counterintuitive.

David then went home and asked for food. He was hungry and wanted to eat. He realized that his fast had not changed the course of the child's illness or death. Did others implore you to eat after the death of your husband or wife? Did you resist, indifferent to their insistence?

"His servants asked him 'Why are you acting this way? While the child was alive, you fasted and wept, but now that the child is dead, you get up and eat!'" (2 Samuel 12:21 NIV). Uncharacteristic behavior is part of grief. It is, in fact, an inalienable right of grief. We are irrational. We scarcely feel sane. We are not ourselves. We may weep uncontrollably and reject the comfort of others. We may refuse to take care of ourselves. The narrative suggests that David returned to his routine easily and quickly. Likely the biblical time line of events is abridged. As his grief subsided, David gradually resumed a semblance of normalcy. He neared *acceptance* of the death of his son. He went on in life to become the second king of the united Kingdom of Israel.

"He answered, 'While the child was still alive, I fasted and wept.' I thought, 'Who knows? The LORD may be gracious to me and let the child live'" (2 Samuel 12:22 NIV). David had a rationale for what he did. His strategy was fasting and weeping as his bargain with God. He was powerless, yet he tried to change the course of the child's illness through self-denial. He dared to imagine that the Lord might heal his child; he hoped in God's grace.

"But now that he is dead, why should I fast? Can I bring him back again? I will go to him, but he will not return to me" (2 Samuel 12:23 NIV). David knew with certainty that the child would not return to him. He was equally certain that he would be with the child again. Likewise, our faith affirms that we will be reunited with those we love who have died, "I will go to him, but he will not return to me." Like David, we trust in the compassionate care of God. In life, as in life beyond death, faith triumphs over every stage of grief.

Suffering

But those who suffer he delivers in their suffering; he speaks to them in their affliction.

—Job 36:15 NIV

Every measure of our capacity to enjoy higher values carries with it a corresponding capacity to suffer. The more highly developed we are, the more sensitive we are. If we did not love, we would not suffer. Generally, we associate suffering with physical distress. When we grieve we suffer the pain of loss. Physical suffering exacerbates grief; grief and suffering are inextricably linked.

Job is the historic paradigm for suffering. "The patience of Job" is a modern idiom. Patience derives from the Latin *patior*, meaning "to suffer." Job patiently suffered affliction, yet he was not entirely passive. He wanted to know the reason; he wanted to know the "why" of his suffering. Job insisted that God meet him face to face and explain the injustice of it all. He expected God to show up and account for himself. Why did God allow Job to suffer? There was never a clear answer. Yet because of his suffering, Job learned to humble himself and trust God.

In grief we seek in vain for the "why" of death. In his book *Cries from the Cross*, Leighton wrote,

> What most of us need in our adversity is not to find an explanation—but to find a victory; it is not to elaborate a theory—but to lay hold upon a power. Even if the best and most completely satisfying answer to our question "why" was available, that would not alter the fact that the actual suffering would still have to be endured. There is a deeper question than "why?" -namely, "how?" The ultimate question is not "Why has this happened to me?" but "How am I to face it?"...Not an explanation of what has happened, but the grace to...bear it.[11]

To suffer is "to bear, allow, let."[12] "Suffer little children to come unto me, and forbid them not: for of such is the kingdom of God" (Luke 18:16 KJV). That is, let the children come, allow them to draw near. As children of God, God calls us into his presence to comfort us in both physical and spiritual suffering. Suffering invites us to place our hurt in larger hands, in God's hands. According to Swiss theologian Hans Küng, "God's love does not protect us *against* all suffering. But it protects us *in* all suffering."[13] Suffering is part of life, part of what it means to be human.

Suffering is also "to endure or bear."[14] As we grieve we suffer attitudes and platitudes intended to comfort that hurt rather than help.

- "God doesn't give you more than you can handle," is loosely based on 1 Corinthians 10:13: "No temptation has seized you except what is common to man. And God is faithful; he will not let you be tempted beyond what you can bear. But when you are tempted, he will also provide a way out so that you can stand up under it it" (NIV). Although temptation is not the same as suffering, the concepts are perhaps interchangeable in the context of grief.
- "It is God's will," explains away the death of our husband or wife as an act of God. This flawed premise denies our right to believe what we believe, to feel what we feel, to grieve as we need to grieve.

Grief specialist Doug Manning states, "God does not gossip.... He does not talk to [others] about you."[15] No matter how convincing others may sound, they do not know the will of God.

At our most vulnerable we suffer familiar secular clichés:

- I understand.
- I know how you feel.
- I know exactly how you feel.

The truth is, no one knows how you feel except you.

We suffer pronouncements meant to console, presumptions that trivialize our grief:

- It's for the best.
- He/she is not suffering anymore.
- He/she is better off.
- He/she is at peace now.
- Everyone dies sooner or later. He/she just died sooner.

We are angry, hurt, and upset when careless comments add to our suffering.

Other statements suggest that our suffering is somehow wrong:

- You shouldn't feel that way.
- Keep a stiff upper lip.
- Be brave.
- Don't cry.

 You should have more faith.

 You ought to give away his/her clothes.

 You'll get over it in a couple of weeks.

 It's time you pull yourself together.

 The children need you to be strong.

 What doesn't kill you makes you stronger.

 You've got to get on with your life.

The unstated directive is "It's time for your suffering to be over." No one knows when that will be; grief does not concede to those urging us to "move on." Friends and family insist that we "get on with our life," yet cannot appreciate that we may never "get over" our grief. We instinctively resist every implied suggestion that we accelerate our return to life.

We suffer "at least" assertions that discount our pain. There is little comfort in empty words:

 At least he/she didn't suffer.

 Things could be worse.

 It's not as bad as it could be.

 Others have had it worse.

 There are worse things than death.

We suffer because we have loved and lost the single most important person in our life. We withdraw and become less communicative for a while, second-guessing our strength and faith. We suffer as long as there is pain as rampant emotions run their course and gradually subside. With unadorned spiritual forbearance we release our pain, and suffering slowly abates. In a sermon on *Grief and Death*, Leighton said, "Suffering is a purifying experience. In losing a part of our lives or something we value, we are given...a clearer view of God. We come through suffering to see things—our lives, especially—not just as they appear, but as they really are."[16]

Suffering leaves an indelible mark on our soul, yet it may be the source of some of the great discoveries of life. It is through suffering that we better understand the thing that really matters: the meaning of faith, hope, and love. It is in suffering that we determine whether our faith is a superficial ornament of life or the essential foundation on which all of life is built. It is in suffering that we can find our deepest experience of God.

If we believe that it is not God's intention that we suffer forever, how do we help ourselves through the suffering of grief?

Prayer

We identify with the humanness of Job: his tears, his doubts, his questions. God knows our feelings. God is never threatened by our emotions, especially those of grief. God longs for us to be open and honest so that we may receive his comfort in this darkest hour of our life. God is trustworthy and understands our grief. We find relief from our suffering when we ask God's help in prayer, when there are no other words than, "Lord, help me" (Matthew 15:25 NRSV).

Patience

There is perhaps no spiritual discipline more difficult than patience. We live in an age that insists on instant gratification and quick results—now. Patience is a gift of grief, a discipline taught by grief. It is listening—"Be still, and know that I am God!" (Psalm 46:10 NRSV). Patience is waiting in faith for God's will to unfold in our life.

Henri Nouwen said that one of the great questions of life has to do not with what happens to us, but with how we will live in and through whatever happens. Our assurance is that God is with us in our suffering and through our suffering. We trust God's promise. "But those who suffer he delivers in their suffering; he speaks to them in their affliction" (Job 36:15 NIV). We will not always suffer.

Stress

⌇

For I am sure that neither death, nor life, nor angels, nor principali-
ties, nor things present, nor things to come, nor powers, nor height,
nor depth, nor anything else in all creation, will be able to separate us
from the love of God in Christ Jesus our Lord.

—*Romans 8:38-39 RSV*

Stress is a ubiquitous malady of contemporary society.

- IBM proclaims in a full page ad, "Today's Special: Stress Relief."
- For $299.00 the StressEraser promises to induce deep meditation by monitoring the heart rate as it charts the pulse with each breath. Tall, regular waves that indicate relaxation score a point towards the desired one hundred per day.
- The Counseling and Mental Health Center at the University of Texas at Austin hosted Stressfest, an afternoon event that show-cased ways for students to relieve pressure and take a break from the stress of academics and campus life. "Stress" and "fest" are at best an oxymoron.

Stress is "hardship, adversity, force, or pressure."[17] Distress is extreme anguish, pain, or suffering. Grief causes stress on both the mind and the body. Grief causes distress in both the heart and the soul. In soul-wrenching moments when life seems hopeless, distress is the worst part of grief.

Stress is highly subjective. It is an emotionally disruptive condition that occurs in response to adverse external influences. It is a psychological and physiological response to events that upset our personal balance. Stress is often cited as a reason for the breakdown of relationships, as a justification for lack of productivity, and as an excuse for unacceptable behavior. It is a blanket rationalization for inertia and general malaise of body, mind, and spirit.

In 1936 Dr. Hans Selye defined stress as "the non-specific response of the body to any demand for change."[18] The stress of grief affects our physical health as increased heart rate, rise in blood pressure, muscular tension, irritability, or depression. A man in the hospital for a heart attack received a call from a concerned staff member at his church. She asked whether the stress of grief for his recently deceased wife might be contributing to his condition. He had not seriously thought of this as a possibility. The question caused him to consider how grief might have physical consequences as well as those of mind and spirit. When we grieve the death of a beloved husband or wife, the body may become ill or break down as a reaction to stress. No effect is without its cause, no cause without its effect.

The Holmes and Rahe Stress Scale[19] assigns a numerical value to these top ten stressful life events:

1. Death of spouse	100
2. Divorce	73
3. Marital separation from mate	65
4. Detention in jail or other institution	63

5. Death of a close family member 63

6. Major personal injury or illness 53

7. Marriage 50

8. Being fired at work 47

9. Marital reconciliation with mate 45

10. Retirement from work 45

The experience of grief can be superimposed on each event:

1. The value assigned to the death of a spouse is 100. It is the most stressful event that can happen in life.

2. The value assigned to divorce drops by over 25 percent. Though the death of our husband or wife is not a legal divorce, grief feels like divorce because the relationship is severed.

3. Marital separation from a mate is the very heart of grief.

4. Grief is at times like imprisonment. The limitations of life without our husband or wife may condemn us to detention in an emotional jail or other institution of our own construct. As we adjust and individuate, our involuntary detention moderates; we no longer feel as confined by the prison of our loss.

5. Your husband or wife was likely your closest family member. Statistically you probably spent the majority of your life with your spouse. You began real adulthood together, creating a home and family apart from your parents.

6. The death of a husband or wife is in every way a major personal injury. For some it may be the cause of illness or physical injury. At the very least, grief is an emotional injury: we are damaged; our heart is broken.

7. Identifying our marital status after the death of a spouse is a stressful process, especially if marriage has been the principal relationship of

our adult life. Are we forever married to our deceased spouse or will we find a new partner and remarry? Do we prefer marriage or learn to live within the framework of a more solitary life?

8. With the death of a husband or wife, we have been fired from our work. We ask, "Who do I cook for, do for, provide for, care for?" "Who will do the same for me?" The event of death summarily fires us from a job that we did so well, that of a devoted spouse. As in the workplace, we chafe at being fired. We are reluctant to pursue a new job, that of finding a purpose in life without our husband or wife.

9. Marital reconciliation with a mate is part of the work of grief. Without the benefit of interactive conversation, reconciliation within ourselves is hard, lonely, stressful work that prolongs our grief.

10. Those who formally retire from the workplace know the sense of accomplishment at a job well done. Yet retirement is often accompanied by the unsettling randomness of finding something else in life to do. In grief we have been retired from our life's work. We live with the daily stress of where to invest our energy, time, and emotional capital, personal resources once dedicated solely to our husband or wife.

SIGNS OF STRESS

- Do you have trouble sleeping?
- Do you overeat or have no appetite?
- Do you worry constantly?
- Do you have increased heart rate or rapid breathing while at rest?
- Are you irritable, angry, or impatient?
- Are you tired?
- Are you unable to concentrate?

The wisdom of the ages, anecdotal reports, numerous clinical studies, and sophisticated testing confirm that a strong social and emotional support system offers relief from stress. Psychiatrist Sidney Cobb defines social support as a subjective sensation in which the individual feels that he or she is cared for and loved, that he or she is esteemed and valued, that he or she belongs to a network of communication and mutual obligation.[20] Social support mitigates the adverse effects of stress on cardiovascular and immune responses. It improves health and prolongs life.

Finally, stress is the scientific principle of physics that explains elasticity, the property that allows matter to resume its original size and shape after being compressed or stretched by an external force. Grief forces us to stretch, almost to the breaking point. The principle of elasticity applies to grief: compressed or stretched by the effect of death, our spirit, in time, resumes its form and shape. The stress of grief is multi-dimensional and real. We triumph over it because we are certain "that neither death, nor life, nor angels, nor principalities, nor things present, nor things to come, nor powers, nor height, nor depth, nor anything else in all creation, will be able to separate us from the love of God in Christ Jesus our Lord" (Romans 8:38-39 RSV).

Rest for Your Soul

*"Come to me, all you that are weary and are carrying heavy burdens,
and I will give you rest. Take my yoke upon you, and learn from me;
for I am gentle and humble in heart, and you will find rest for your
souls. For my yoke is easy, and my burden is light."*

—*Matthew 11:28-30 NRSV*

Grief is work. It is a full-time job, a 24/7 occupation. It is physically
exhausting to grieve. The things of this world necessitate physical
chores that layer grief with fatigue. Duties and responsibilities once
shared are now ours alone. Grief demands our energy; it appropriates our
personal reserves and it depletes our emotional resources. When grief is
at the forefront of every thought and action, it is almost unimaginable to
let it go. Self-nurture mandates that we lay aside our grief to rest from
time to time.

Grief is a tireless companion on our journey through the valley of the
shadow of death. If you have ever traveled to an activity destination that
was more exhausting than relaxing, or been on a trip that felt more like
work than pleasure, the moment comes when we must rest. We cannot
drive one more mile or sleep in one more uncomfortable bed. We stop at

a nearby motel, or hurry home to reach the comfort of our familiar environment. In grief, as on all arduous journeys, our body and spirit demand that we rest.

We move forward in grief, yet setbacks are inevitable. We must rest before we try again. When they occur, setbacks feel like a complete undoing of our hard-won progress, one step forward then two steps back. We rest. Gains in grief are slow and incremental. Slowly, imperceptibly grief becomes two steps forward and one step back. We grieve forward; we rest.

We rest from grief when we release our emotions through tears. There is scientific evidence that crying releases endorphins, brain chemicals that function as pain relievers and mood elevators. Because tears are cathartic, we usually feel better after we have had a good cry. There are times when we have cried so much that we feel physically spent, all in, at the end of our resources. This is the moment to rest.

- Tears are the expression of the deep feelings that reside beneath the surface of our fragile exterior, those that words cannot express. When words fail, tears are the messenger.
- Tears are cleansing. They wash away some of the emotions that trouble us in grief. Tears are honest. Denying our tears prevents us from working though pain.
- Tears are healing. Crying releases tension and physical distress.

> *God will wipe away every tear from their eyes; and death shall be no more, neither shall there be anguish [sorrow and mourning] nor grief nor pain any more . . .*
>
> *—Revelation 21:4 AMP*

"Come to me all you that are weary and are carrying heaven burdens, and I will give you rest" (Matthew 11:28 NRSV). When we grieve, we are weary because the burden of it all seems unbearably heavy. The Message Bible states it this way, "Are you tired? Worn out? Come to me. Get away with me and you'll recover your life. I'll show you how to take a real rest. Walk with me and work with me—watch how I do it. Learn the unforced rhythms of grace." To recover your life, you must get away with God. God's promise to you is rest. God invites you to learn "the unforced rhythms of grace," wherein you will find rest for your soul. "Take my yoke upon you, and learn from me; for I am gentle and humble in heart, and you will find rest for your souls" (Matthew 11:29 NRSV).

We receive our best insights when we listen to the still and quiet within our hearts that is rest.

- rest for the body
- rest for the mind
- rest for the heart
- rest for the soul
- rest from grief

We put down our load for a while, but like any faithful companion, grief waits while we rest. When we return, it will be there waiting for us, though not as insistent as before. Rest. Find rest for your soul. "Come to me, all you that are weary and are carrying heavy burdens, and I will give you rest. Take my yoke upon you, and learn from me; for I am gentle and humble in heart, and you will find rest for your souls" (Matthew 11:28-30 NRSV).

Courage

⸻

We are hard pressed on every side, but not crushed; perplexed, but not in despair; persecuted, but not abandoned; struck down, but not destroyed.

—*2 Corinthians 4:8-9 NIV*

The media frequently report a human interest story of courage and bravery in which the ordinary becomes extraordinary.

- A small child is rescued by a young sibling.
- Two firemen pull a driver from a burning car.
- An elderly person is saved from a house fire.
- A vital organ is donated to save the life of another person.
- Terrorists are subdued even as brave men and women perish in a plane crash for the sake of the greater good, as on 9/11/2001.
- A pilot lands an aircraft safely in the Hudson River and saves 155 lives.

Courage is heroic and inspiring. The word *courage* is derived from the Latin *cor*, meaning "heart." The cry "Courage!" is often used to stirring effect in theater productions as a call to strength and bold action. Henri Nouwen wrote, "To have courage is to listen to our heart, to speak from our heart, and to act from our heart. Our heart, which is the center of our being, is the seat of courage."[21] Courage is an outward response to our inner fear. Courage is our fear turned inside out. When we transform fear into courage by doing that which we fear, we become stronger. In grief we simultaneously deconstruct fear and reconstruct courage.

"We are hard pressed on every side, but not crushed; perplexed, but not in despair; persecuted, but not abandoned; struck down, but not destroyed" (2 Corinthians 4:8-9 NIV). Our very will to survive is hard-pressed by grief. Yet we are not crushed. When sorrow overwhelms us, faith in the steadfast love of God fortifies our courage. We are hard pressed, but we are not crushed by grief.

We are perplexed by the never-to-be answered questions about the death of our husband or wife.

- Why?
- Why me?
- Why didn't God answer my prayers for healing with "yes"?
- Why did this have to happen now?
- Why did he/she have to die and not me?
- How can I go on without my husband or wife?

For a while, questions are the constant theme of our chaotic thoughts. We want answers because we are perplexed. In dark moments we tiptoe to the precipice of despair and peek over the edge into the darkness of depression, only to behold the vast mystery of death. Yet through faith we have courage to trust the unknown. We are perplexed but we do not despair.

We may feel persecuted or punished by the death of our husband or wife. Our unresolved emotions, guilt, or a sense of responsibility for what happened may drive the effect of persecution and punishment. God expands the boundaries of our courage beyond a momentary sense of persecution or punishment. God is with us as we grieve.

When we are unable to function because of anguish and distress, we are struck down for a while emotionally and perhaps spiritually. Or we may be felled physically by unanticipated illness or infirmity. When we courageously rekindle our life from the ashes of sorrow, we acknowledge with gratitude that we have not been destroyed by the death of our husband or wife. Life is forever changed and life will never be the same. Yet we survive. The assurance of life beyond death empowers us to live with courage. We are struck down but not destroyed.

The spirit that enables us to face difficulty without fear is bravery. Bravery is the bold, intrepid courage inspired by the love of God, our citadel, the bastion of our faith. In grief, bravery may be weak and tentative, yet when we dare those conscious acts that test our courage, our faith is rewarded in dividends of self-confidence and hope. In his book *The Life Triumphant: Mastering the Heart and Mind*, James Allen writes, "For those who will fight bravely and not yield, there is triumphant victory over all the dark things of life."[22]

When we fight bravely and succeed, we experience within the victory that deserves a medal as an outward acknowledgment of our courage. In courage we venture from our place of pervasive woundedness to gradually rejoin the world with renewed strength. Acts of brute courage require bravery to defeat the persistent fears of grief:

- Have you returned to church, awkwardly aware of your bravery as you attend without your spouse?
- Have you gotten in the car for a road trip alone?
- Have you travelled to a familiar or new destination and found the courage to conquer and grow?

☙ Have you had a medical procedure or surgery that was daunting without your husband or wife at your side, holding your hand, loving you, reassuring you?

☙ Have you made the decision to make a major change in life, whether tearing out a wall, moving to a new home, or remarriage?

As we grieve we seek the best part of courage: *encouragement*. When we share with others who have experienced the death of a beloved husband or wife, we recognize that we are not alone. We are encouraged by community, in communion with others who grieve. "May...God our Father, who loved us and by his grace gave us eternal encouragement and good hope, encourage your hearts and strengthen you in every good deed and word" (2 Thessalonians 2:16-17 NIV). In courage we are reborn as we slowly find the way back into life. As we receive the promise of eternal encouragement and good hope we begin to live again, resurrected from grief. "We are hard pressed on every side, but not crushed; perplexed, but not in despair; persecuted, but not abandoned; struck down, but not destroyed" (2 Corinthians 4:8-9 NIV).

☙ What are your fears that need to be expressed as courage?

☙ Who or what gives you encouragement?

☙ What acts of courage have transformed your experience of grief?

☙ What is the source of your spiritual encouragement?

Attitude

So I tell you this...that you must no longer live as the Gentiles do, in the futility of their thinking. They are darkened in their understanding and separated from the life of God because of the ignorance that is in them due to the hardening of their hearts. . . . You were taught . . . to put off your old self . . . to be made new in the attitude of your minds; and to put on the new self, created to be like God in true righteousness and holiness.

—Ephesians 4:17-18, 22-24 NIV

The experience of most people in grief is that life seems out of control on many levels. We exist for a while in a dense fog. Our best judgment is impaired by unfamiliar mental chaos, distraction, and confusion. We lack information and understanding, which is often the cause of our fear, anxiety, and helplessness. We learn through the experience of grief that we are not in control of the circumstances, either of life or death.

The fact is that the only thing you can truly control in grief is your attitude. Everything precious including your dignity can be taken from you but the one thing that cannot be taken away is your power to choose what attitude you will take toward the events that have happened.

Through the right attitude, unchangeable suffering is changed into a heroic and victorious achievement.

Austrian neurologist and psychiatrist Victor Frankl, a Holocaust survivor, believed that we find meaning in life within our attitude toward suffering. In his bestselling book *Man's Search for Meaning,* he relates this experience:

> Once, an elderly general practitioner consulted me because of his severe depression. He could not overcome the loss of his wife who had died two years before and whom he had loved above all else. I confronted him with the question, "What would have happened, Doctor, if you had died first, and your wife would have had to survive you?" "Oh," he said, "For her this would have been terrible; how she would have suffered!" Whereupon I replied, "You see, Doctor, such suffering has been spared her, and it was you who have spared her this suffering—to be sure, at the price that now you have to survive and mourn her." He said no word but shook my hand and calmly left my office. In some way, suffering ceases to be suffering at the moment it finds a meaning, such as the meaning of a sacrifice.
>
> Of course, this was no therapy in the proper sense since, first, his despair was no disease; and second, I could not change his fate; I could not revive his wife. But in that moment I did succeed in changing his attitude toward his unalterable fate inasmuch as from that time on he could at least see a meaning in his suffering.[23]

For a while we must feel what we feel; grief is both power and presence. With only the will to breathe, we struggle to survive. As shock fades, we name anger, fear, worry, and loneliness with unaccustomed emotional honesty. The work of grief is reconciling our attitude about what happened to change our life with the reality of life as it is becoming.

Frankl, who was intimately acquainted with tragedy and suffering, made this bold affirmation: "Even the helpless victim of a hopeless situation, facing a fate he cannot change, may rise above himself, may grow beyond himself, and by so doing change himself. He may turn a personal tragedy into a triumph."[24] When grief at last releases its insistent hold on our heart and mind, we reach a turning point: we begin to think again, clearly, rationally. We realize that we cannot change what happened. At last we understand that our attitude is fluid, shaped by the perspective of our grief journey.

As we better understand grief on the upward climb out of the valley of the shadow of death, renewed confidence quietly becomes a positive attitude. We embrace this fundamental truth: *life is worth living.*

Our attitude toward the death of our husband or wife is a choice emboldened by faith, or one that is a measure of faith:

- Do you choose to live in seclusion, isolated and alone?
- Do you choose to blame others, embittered and angry towards those who "caused" or did nothing to prevent the death of your husband or wife?
- Do you choose to torment yourself because you could not save his or her life?
- Do you choose to immerse yourself in self-pity, in quiet defiance of the world at large?

The explanation for our attitude runs deep. We have loved and been truly loved in the sacred bond of marriage. Those blessed with a soul mate, the embodied match of our own immortal soul, know the symmetry and fine balance of man to woman. God-ordained soul mates are like a durable fabric of sturdy weft and warp with threads of trust and respect interwoven at perfect right angles, the complement of vertical to horizontal, of husband to wife. Leighton and I were true once-in-a-lifetime soul mates committed to an indestructible partnership. We celebrated each day and lived with passion, as though any moment might be our last. When you have lost your soul mate in death, you grieve because you have loved and been truly loved.

The death of our soul mate informs our choice of attitude. When we look into sorrow we glimpse not only the emptiness of loss, but also the reflection of our own spirit. Recently I sat at dinner with a friend who remarked on how much I had given to Leighton. I seldom think of any influence or effect I may have had on my husband's life. My memory suggests that he did all the giving. Yet in that moment my spirit lifted, my heart warmed, and my attitude changed as I looked beyond my own sorrow to see from the perspective of another my contribution to Leighton's life.

Our heart is transformed and our attitude refined when we appreciate that we have given in equal measure our own best gifts to our husband or wife. The reflected love, which abides eternally within, is the mirror image of our soul mate. In *Safe Passage*, Molly Fumia writes, "Rest assured that in her dying, in her flight through darkness toward a new light, she held you in her arms and carried your closeness with her. And when she arrived at God, your image was imprinted on her joy-filled soul."[25] When we realize that within ourselves shines the eternal, reflected spirit of our husband or wife, we choose attitudes that honor and bless the memory of our beloved. The soul mate attitude carries us forward into whatever the future may hold.

> *So I tell you this . . . that you must no longer live as the Gentiles do, in the futility of their thinking. They are darkened in their understanding and separated from the life of God because of the ignorance that is in them due to the hardening of their hearts....You were taught...to put off your old self...to be made new in the attitude of your minds; and to put on the new self, created to be like God in true righteousness and holiness.*
>
> —*Ephesians 4:17-18, 22-24 NIV*

When the heart is intractable, hardened by the pain of death, our grief is well described as ignorance, futility of thinking, darkness of understanding, and separation from God. To put off our old self and be made new in the attitude of our mind is the endeavor of grief. Our old self may be a weary, emotionally tattered half-person, as familiar and comfortable as an old bathrobe. What happens to our old self when our husband or wife dies? As we assimilate grief we discover that we are becoming different people. Never again will we be the person we once were.

To be made new in the attitude of our mind is to find a new self. We choose whether we put on our new self and wear it gladly, or whether we shrug into it with reluctance. We try it on for size and make adjustments before we are satisfied with the fit. Grief enlarges us to accommodate a new self—a different self, a better self.

In her novel *Adam Bede*, George Eliot wrote these poignant words:

> For Adam . . . had not outlived his sorrow—had not felt it slip from him as a temporary burden, and leave him the same man again. Do any of us? God forbid. It would be a poor result of all our anguish and our wrestling, if we won nothing but our old selves at the end of it—if we could return to the same blind loves, the same self-confident blame, the same light thoughts of human suffering, the same frivolous gossip over blighted human lives, the same feeble sense of that Unknown towards which we have sent forth irrepressible cries in our loneliness. Let us rather be thankful that sorrow lives in us as an indestructible force, only changing its form, as forces do, and passing from pain into sympathy—the one poor word which includes all our best insight and our best love.[26]

A grateful heart has within it the embryo of a new self. The attitude that defines our new self is directed by gratitude for the one we have lost and gratitude for what we have left. Attitude is a choice, "put off your old self . . . be made new in the attitude of your minds . . . put on the new self" (Ephesians 4:22-24 NIV).

Victim or Survivor

"For I know the plans I have for you," declares the LORD, "plans to
prosper you and not to harm you, plans to give you hope and a future."
—Jeremiah 29:11 NIV

A victim is "one that is made to suffer injury, loss, or death."[27] With
the death of our husband or wife we become a victim, through no
action of our own. As victims we may feel abandoned by God or by the
one who died. Indeed, a sense of abandonment is a real part of victimization, yet we are never abandoned by God.

Our life seems irreparably damaged by the permanent loss of our husband or wife. We are helpless to change the effect that death has on our
life because our emotional, physical, and spiritual reserves are compromised, depleted by the demands of grief. Especially when we experience
the untimely or premature death of a beloved spouse, our self-perception
is that of a frustrated, powerless victim. We are unprepared to manage our
victimization because for a while we can concentrate on nothing except
the pain of grief.

Victimization may be a place on the grief journey where we reside for
a while. It is important to acknowledge our sense of victimization, but not

to succumb to anger or powerlessness, thereby allowing death to claim more than its share of our life. When we own our sense of victimization, we reach a significant crossroad on our journey toward life beyond the death of our husband or wife.

When circumstances compel us to abandon our victimization before adequately working through thoughts and feelings about what happened, we forfeit an important part of grief. Someone or something may expect you to function and cope despite your grief, forcing you to live beyond victimization before you have sufficiently honored your grief. The urgency of a job, children, grandchildren, aging parents, or any other combination of non-negotiable demands may distract you from your need to grieve. The effect may be to postpone grief for months or even years. Grief can be delayed, but it will not be denied.

We are loyal to ourselves when we refuse to give up any part of the grief experience necessary for the survival of our soul and spirit. We sustain victimization when social controls dictate our actions. Social controls insist that we conform to the demands of the society in which we live.

- Do you betray your grief by putting on a façade that denies your true emotions?
- Do you suppress your tears, feigning a smile that belies your broken heart?
- Do you feel pressured by others to rejoin life before you have fully engaged with your loss?
- Does giving in for the comfort of others feel like giving up on grief?

The following "survival strategies" may help with managing the victimization of grief:[28]

- Face being alone
- Name your thoughts and feelings
- Allow others to see your tears
- Ask for help—family, friends, clergy, therapist
- Avoid toxic, angry, or judgmental people, and those who want to control
- Dress and go outside each day
- Talk to another person each day
- Move your body—exercise in small ways
- Eat at least one healthy meal each day
- Perform only safe tasks that do not exceed your concentration level
- Avoid excessive use of alcohol and/or drugs
- Spend as little money as possible
- Take care of your health needs because grief affects the immune system

Beyond these survival strategies, we can consciously resolve to survive. The choice is surviving day-to-day or surviving for life. If we are empowered rather than debilitated by the experience of life and death, we want to survive, to be a Survivor–*capital S.*

Death forever alters those who survive. Our identity and worldview change. In death we lose our husband or wife; in grief we lose the person we were when they were alive. With the death of our spouse we lose the assumptions upon which life was built and our vision of the future. As survivors, we see the world for a while through a haze of sadness, but ultimately our place in the future will come back into view.

Moving from victim to Survivor is a milestone in grief. We herald this signal moment of personal triumph as we dare to survive in fullness of life. We are Survivors because we believe God's unconditional declaration, "'For I know the plans I have for you,' declares the LORD, 'plans to prosper you and not to harm you, plans to give you hope and a future'" (Jeremiah 29:11 NIV).

Where Do I Fit in Life?

Do not worry about anything, but in everything by prayer and supplication with thanksgiving let your requests be made known to God. And the peace of God, which surpasses all understanding, will guard your hearts and your minds in Christ Jesus.

—Philippians 4:6-7 NRSV

As we grieve we ask, *Where do I fit in life?* The dangling, pain-filled end of the question implies *without my husband or wife.* We struggle to make sense of life alone without our partner.

Where do I fit in life? is the question that embodies much of our anxiety.

Our social self-perception is that of being somehow "less than" because of the absence of our husband or wife. Through attrition we may feel that we have been involuntarily demoted to "second-class citizen," which is defined as one who is not accorded a fair share of respect, recognition, or consideration. When we reject inferior labels, we assert our place in the world, affirming our individuality as we readjust to fit in life.

Recently I observed a distinguished-looking gentleman in a grocery store, a community leader admired for his wealth and social standing whose wife had died a few months earlier. This titan of industry was clearly overwhelmed, evidently perplexed by the task of shopping. He looked uncomfortable and strangely forlorn. Really, he seemed rather pitiful. Because Leighton had known him personally, I ventured to speak. The man seemed relieved that someone would acknowledge that he was not invisible. His entire demeanor suggested the anxiety of a second-class citizen as he attempted to navigate the large, unfamiliar store. The death of our husband or wife may imperil our self-confidence. With considerable consternation we wonder, "Where do I fit in life?"

As human beings we want to be treated with respect. When we are suddenly single we may ask, "Where do I fit in life?"—especially when we are not accorded the same respect as when we were part of a couple. We feel somehow discounted because of our loss. Have you experienced moments of awkwardness when invited to join married friends you enjoyed together before the death of your spouse? Our social reality is the loss of our husband or wife. The comfortable place within the social structure of others we enjoyed as a couple has changed.

Moments when we are a "fifth wheel" accentuate our aloneness. Physically we are no longer part of a couple. Have you been seated at a table across from an empty chair that is the strong visual reminder of the one absent? When others are unexpectedly thoughtless or inconsiderate we ask yet again, "Where do I fit in life?"

Developing our self-perception as a worthwhile, stand-alone individual is a formidable hurdle of grief. As we transition through grief, we re-individuate. Or perhaps we truly individuate for the first time in life as we discover our identity without reference to our husband or wife. We begin to appreciate the personal, God-given qualities uniquely our own and begin to explore possibilities beyond our own imagination.

Anxious moments occur as we adjust to fit into the life of our children, who are now without a father or mother. Rebalancing relationships within a permanently altered family structure is an emotional complication of grief. Your children may make an effort to include you in their lives, yet your role as parent without the equal and opposite presence of your husband or wife is changed and imperceptibly redefined.

Your children may perceive you as more dependent and in need of a substitute husband or wife, a role you neither desire nor want them to fulfill. You may feel ignored or hurt if they presume on your strength when in fact you need their support. In turn, they feel inadequate to satisfy your emotional and physical needs. Interpersonal relationships are complicated; each individual family has its own dynamic.

Cast all your anxiety on him, because he cares for you.
—*1 Peter 5:7 NRSV*

We cast off our anxieties for a while, yet as humans we reserve the right to take them back. Again you may ask, "Where do I fit in life?" When we grieve it is difficult to abandon our anxieties and relax into God's loving care. Casting is a decisive, conscious act; it is more than just putting our anxieties aside.

If you fish or know someone who does, you have seen firsthand the exquisite moment of release that is casting. In one fluid, smooth motion the delicate line soars upward and outward into space. It hovers over the surface for an instant, then floats above it as though suspended in space, and inevitably falls into the water, descending with grace into the unknown depths. Imagine your anxieties on the end of the line, soaring God-ward through the air. Casting is letting go, allowing God to calm, relieve, and transform us when we release our anxieties to God's care.

Again and yet again we ask, "Where do I fit in life?" God understands our grief-driven anxiety about our new place in the social structure of life.

God promises peace to sustain us through our grief: "Have no anxiety about anything, but in everything by prayer and supplication with thanksgiving let your requests be made known to God. And the peace of God, which passes all understanding, will keep your hearts and your minds in Christ Jesus" (Philippians 4:6-7 RSV). When we are at peace, restored from within to a life of full citizenship, we again fit in to life with renewed strength and rediscovered self-confidence.

Make the Effort

Let us therefore make every effort to do what leads to peace and mutual edification.

—Romans 14:19 NIV

Over seventeen years of marriage, Leighton and I attempted to blend our acquired families. We wanted to create the harmonious, loving circle of a new family, "our" family, from a disparate group that ranged in age from newborn to seventy. We never succeeded, yet we had a slogan, "Really, we really try really hard, really." We tried hard. We made an effort.

Life takes an effort, whatever the circumstance or quest. Grief demands that we make an effort in order to survive. The scripture says, "Let us therefore *make every effort* to do what leads to peace and mutual edification." As we make the effort to better understand grief, we grow in our capacity for peace and mutual edification. What is mutual edification? It is the encouragement and comfort we experience when we share our grief with others who understand and care.

The assumption of grief is that we are supposed to "do" something to help ourselves. Effort and trying are the assumptions of doing. At first, all we want to do is succumb to heartbreak. This is the right time in grief to do nothing. The body dictates our limitations; it insists that we rest. We must do nothing for a while to recover physically from the initial phase of grief that is emotional trauma and shock.

At the pool of Bethesda in Jerusalem, an angel of the Lord came down from time to time to stir up the waters. The first one into the pool after each such disturbance would be cured of whatever disease he had. A man sitting beside the pool had been an invalid for thirty-eight years. When asked, "Do you want to get well?" he replied, "I have no one to help me into the pool when the water is stirred. While I am trying to get in, some-one else goes down ahead of me" (John 5:6-7 NIV). He wanted to be healed, but physically he was helpless. He was unable to manage his infirm body into the pool by himself. His effort was not enough to get ahead of others who were more mobile or able-bodied.

Similarly, we are challenged by the death of our husband or wife to try in new, unaccustomed ways to "get into the pool."

- You try to find where you fit in life without your husband or wife.
- You try to adjust to single life.
- You "try on" new ways to live, perhaps alone for the first time in life.
- You "try out" new people or routines.
- You try to adapt to the expectations of others.
- You try new experiences.
- You try to go on with life.

Trying may feel like failure or like unexpected success. In fact, trying may feel like a full-time occupation. Yet every small victory is progress in grief. There are no real failures when we try.

A new friend whose husband had died called unexpectedly one Sunday afternoon. She asked if I would go to a concert with her at the church that evening because she was tired of sitting at home alone. She was trying to connect, to break through her own isolation and solitude by doing something uplifting and social. She was trying to change her life for at least one evening.

Our place as a vital member of society, as a contributor to humanity, is now perhaps unfamiliar because we are alone. Trying is using our talents and interests to give to others. Trying is using our unique, God-given gifts and graces in service to others. Trying is using our personal expertise to go beyond ourselves in grief. Trying means making the effort to stay connected to the world, a world that is not waiting on us, or for us.

There is no guarantee that effort alone will ease the void in our heart once filled by the love and energy of our husband or wife. It will always matter to us that we have loved and lost; it will never *not* matter. Because it matters less to the world, we must make the effort to accommodate life as it surrounds us. This is a responsibility of grief.

We honor our husband or wife when we reenter the world and endow others with our spirit. Our reentry may unfold gradually in small increments, or there may be a moment of personal resolve to try. When we acknowledge that our life is here, and now, and at this place, we find ourselves more willing to make the effort.

If making an effort seems consistently overwhelming, it may be time to seek the help of a confidential, non-judgmental counselor, therapist, or minister who will listen thoughtfully to understand your grief. The guidance of a qualified professional may be critical for moving forward in grief.

Making an effort and trying are "doing" actions that stretch us. When we stretch in grief, we grow. We grow toward God. We grow in affirmation of life. We grow in the assurance that we are not alone. Our charge in grief is to try, to "make every effort to do what leads to peace and mutual edification" (Romans 14:19 NIV). Make the effort. Try.

Gender-Specific Grief

A father to the fatherless, a defender of widows, is God in his holy dwelling.

—*Psalm 68:5 NIV*

Jesus wept.

—*John 11:35 NIV*

Statistically, women live longer than men. In our society, there are more widows than widowers. Grief literature and support groups are typically biased toward women; men are remarkably underserved. A mistaken presumption of male grief is that men are brave and strong and do not hurt as much as women.

In the Bible, there are dozens of verses that refer to widows, usually in the context of care and compassion. Widows were outcasts, at the mercy of their families for sustenance and livelihood. The book of Ruth is the story of three widows, two young and one old. It relates how they respond to the loss of their husbands, and how God blessed each in a unique way.

The emotional needs of a man with a broken heart are often neglected when a husband survives his wife. There is little reference in the Bible to the grief of men. Following the death of a wife, men were expected to remarry and continue the family lineage. "Widower" was a temporary status.

Upon hearing the news that his friend Lazarus had died, Jesus was "greatly disturbed in spirit and deeply moved" (John 11:33b NRSV). He had not been there when Lazarus died, as he might have been. His emotions were in turmoil; he expressed his pain and sorrow in heartfelt grief: "Jesus wept" (John 11:35 NIV). Jesus showed unqualified emotion as he grieved his friend. The people who observed his grief said, "See how he loved him!" (John 11:36 NRSV).

We know that Jesus was manly. He was a man's man whose primary company was twelve other men. The Bible offers no explanation for his tears and no apology for his heartfelt outpouring of grief. Love is the universal reason that we grieve.

We love our husband or wife so intimately and dearly that tears are our purest expression of loss and human pain. Women typically feel more comfortable crying—tears of both sadness and joy. In contrast, men are discouraged from tearful self-expression. One of the special things I cherish about Leighton is that he cried at movies. He was not ashamed to cry and express emotion. Men should weep when their heart is broken. They should cry when a beloved wife dies and leaves them unexpectedly alone. Jesus wept. There is no greater example for men who grieve.

For a surviving husband, the death of a wife may result in social disconnection that leads to isolation, loneliness, and depression. This is one of the most difficult aspects of grief for men. Most women are networked for emotional support through family and friends. In a marriage, the wife typically instigates and facilitates most relationships. It is an extra burden of grief for men to sustain meaningful contact with others without their wives.

Many who have lost a spouse struggle with the designations "widow" and "widower," which to some suggest resignation from life and loss of a future. In the more modern world in which we live, these words qualify as social controls for those who have experienced the death of a husband or wife. For many survivors, these words may feel old-fashioned or dated.

Some women express helplessness or mild resentment about assuming many responsibilities their husbands may have handled exclusively or primarily, jobs often considered "man's work":

- managing finances
- doing business
- earning a living
- having the car serviced
- keeping the house in repair
- interacting with service providers

Likewise, many practicalities of daily living can be an ongoing struggle for men, such as:

- meal preparation
- eating alone
- doing the laundry
- care of a house that no longer feels like a home without a wife's loving presence

> *We . . . rejoice in our sufferings, knowing that suffering produces endurance, and endurance produces character, and character produces hope.*
>
> —*Romans 5:3-4 ESV*

This scripture speaks very personally about grief, whether to a man or woman. We suffer because we have loved and lost our husband or wife; we endure it because life demands that we live in the present. And after we have suffered for a while, enduring through grief, we are rewarded with fortified character inspired by hope. As men and women of faith, we dare to hope because we believe that in life and in death, and in life beyond death, God is with us. Thanks be to God that we are not alone.

Change and Growth

Blessed is the man who perseveres under trial, because when he has stood the test, he will receive the crown of life that God has promised to those who love him. . . . Every good and perfect gift is from above, coming down from the Father of the heavenly lights, who does not change like shifting shadows.

—James 1:12, 17 NIV

The directional arrow on a prominently displayed sign indicates that a neighborhood church has moved a few blocks north. It proclaims, "We've grown. We've moved." Simple words convey the message. Something happened; things changed. Because of the death of our husband or wife, everything changes.

When we grieve, we resist every change thrust upon us by the death of our spouse. From the lessons of life we learn that change is the constant of time. But we are assured that God is the one thing that does not change, "the Father of the heavenly lights, who does not change like shifting shadows" (James 1:17 NIV). Grief is our "shifting shadow."

The experience of death teaches us that the ordinary is precious. Through the heartache and sorrow of grief we better understand that our days together with our husband or wife were a treasure. Author Mitch Albom observed, "We often fantasize about a perfect day, but when it comes to those we miss, we desperately want one more familiar meal, even one more argument."[29] When we grieve we yearn for the ordinary and we desperately want the familiar. In his poem "To a Skylark," Shelley reflects, "We look before and after, and pine for what is not."[30] We want life to be the same as it once was. We want our life back. The hard reality of grief is that nothing will ever be the same again because everything has changed.

From the first bad news of illness, accident, or sudden death, grief becomes an active participant in our life. It may feel like an ominous cloud of eternal darkness. But grief is more a shifting shadow, one that obscures all of life for a while then whispers away as it passes.

Grief shifts as you experience certain inevitabilities that affirm the reality of the death of your spouse. You attend a probate hearing. You settle his or her estate. You attend to the disposition of your husband or wife's worldly things. In these "shifting shadow" moments we are forced by the business of life to face our loss. As reality dawns, shock slips away. We feel our grief is naked and exposed. We learn that grief is both adapting to change and growing into change.

Grief modulates as gradually its power to direct our every mood and moment subsides. We create space for its co-existence within the confines of an irrevocably changed life. And as grief changes, it is reframed to include the steady presence of our husband or wife, safely ensconced forever in our heart. Though grief may linger in some small corner of our heart forever, we are sustained by our memories, which are the most precious and sacred part of the past. We will never, ever forget.

As shadows shift, death no longer defines our existence. It is what happened to change our life forever. There is no benefit to reliving the past because the outcome will always be the same. Yet scraps of memory will always float up and around us to remind and assure us that the past was real. Our earthly life together happened. Nothing can void or erase that which we had in our married lifetime together. The reason is that love remains. Our love will always be. This will never change. When shadows shift, light shines through.

Inherent in grief is its power to change us. Grief can impact us negatively or positively.

Grief can make us:

Stronger	or	Weaker	or	Embittered
More Faithful	or	Disillusioned	or	Spiritually Isolated
More Capable	or	Disabled	or	Dysfunctional
Independent	or	Dependent	or	Helpless
Wiser	or	Stubborn	or	Willful
Deliberate	or	Impulsive	or	Rash

🕊 How has your grief changed?

🕊 How has grief changed you?

Change offers two possibilities. We grow, or we remain rooted in a physical and emotional past that no longer exists. To grow or not to grow is the central choice of grief. We are forced to change, but we choose whether we grow. When we grow, we claim life moving forward. When we resist, we succumb to the past, spending our days in frustration and self-pity. We grow spiritually when we allow change to propel us away from the past toward new life. "Old things are passed away; behold, all things are become new" (2 Corinthians 5:17 KJV).

🕊 What old things seem 'passed away' from life because of the death of your husband or wife?

- Have old relationships died?
- Are people, places, or experiences of your life together now part of the past, "passed away" from your life?

Like the words on the sign, our life now declares, "We've grown. We've moved." Something happened; things have changed. We are called to grow. We choose to grow. Life continues to unfold when we dare to grow. Growth moves us to a new place in life that inspires our reinvestment in the future. Our faith emboldens us to grow and change through the experience of grief. Our hope is in "the Father of the heavenly lights, who does not change like shifting shadows" (James 1:17 NIV).

PART II

Beyond the Broken Heart

Durable Love

Love knows no limit to its endurance, no end to its trust, no fading of its hope; it can outlast anything. It is, in fact, the one thing that still stands when all else has fallen.

—*1 Corinthians 13:7-8 JBP*

Why do we grieve? We grieve because we love. This is the answer to the "why" of our pain. We grieve in direct proportion to the depth of our love. The more we love, the greater our grief. The ratio of love to loss does not depend on the duration of a marriage. It depends rather on the depth of our relationship measured by the quality of our love. Few of us would forego love to avoid the pain of grief. Even in the face of grief we give thanks for having loved so deeply that when death touches our lives, we can do nothing for a while except grieve. Love is the one thing that still stands when all else has fallen.

The spiritual basis for the reality of durable love is found in the assurance that "God is love" (1 John 4:16a NRSV). If we know that God is love and that God ordains love, then we believe that love can outlast anything. The love of our husband and wife for us transcends the event of death. This is the absolute power of love.

In marriage we create a legacy of love that begs to be given away with abandon. Our shared legacy of love is part of who we are, available to lavish on those we love and on those in need of hope and encouragement.

- ❧ What do we do with our earthly, mortal love?
- ❧ How do we care for it?
- ❧ How do we nurture it?
- ❧ How do we spend it?

Though love is turned upside down and inside out by the death of our husband or wife, we quickly discern, to our great comfort, that our shared love lives on—and on and on—when we invest in others. William Barclay has written, "When we spend ourselves to help those in trouble, in distress, in pain, in sorrow, in affliction, God is using us as the highway by which he sends his help into the lives of his people. To help another person in need is to manifest the glory of God, for it is to show what God is like."[31]

We grow spiritually when we reach out to comfort and help another in grief by giving our love away with compassion and understanding. When we embrace others who are grieving the loss of a beloved husband or wife, we offer them the emotional and spiritual authenticity of a profound shared experience as we reach out in word or deed to say, "I hurt with you; I share your pain; I love you." According to American Christian theologian Robert McAfee Brown, "Death by itself may not encourage connections. It may simply drive home more deeply the solitude of loss. But love encourages, and even builds connections, and there is no way to separate love and death."[32] Love never fails, it can outlast anything.

Where does human sexuality fit into the complex of grief? As human beings we are created to give and receive gratification as a physical expression of love in marriage. Through no fault of our own, the status of widow or widower has a slightly asexual connotation, which is also a very real part of grief. For some the need for physical affection and companionship may be overwhelming, requited by compromise or premature remarriage. We manage this void in our life as we channel our physical and emotional energies and slowly come to terms with a more solitary physical existence.

Leighton and I had an intensely physical relationship. I miss his hand holding mine every minute, the romance, the exquisite love of it all. Physical, mental, and emotional intimacy was a powerful force in what was truly a God-ordained marriage. Our bond was so strong and close it felt like a part of me died when he died. Many widows and widowers have the same feeling of being only half alive when a physical relationship is ended by death. Yet love can outlast anything, even sexual deprivation.

Life together in that time and space shared in a relationship of love with our husband or wife is both fragile and eternal. Because love can outlast anything, the inner sanctum we shared with our spouse is sacred. It remains fully intact, never diminished. It will always be part of who we are, whatever the future. No one can take it away and nothing can destroy it. At first we desperately hold on then slowly we realize that nothing is lost or compromised if we release our tenacious emotional grip and relax into the certainty that love is. If we invite another into our life to be our life's partner or spouse, a new place will be added alongside that which belongs forever to the one we now grieve. In *Sonnets from the Portuguese*, Elizabeth Barrett Browning wrote, "I love thee with the breath, smiles, tears, of all my life. And, if God choose, I shall but love thee better after death."[33] The truth about love is this: the more there is, the more there is to give away. Love can outlast anything.

The love that we have known with our husband or wife here on earth will never die. It is eternal. Death has not taken it away; it has only separated us in body, but not in heart. The grace of God is the very essence of love in our life. Love can outlast anything.

The Faithfulness of God

O LORD, you are my God; I will exalt you and praise your name, for in perfect faithfulness you have done marvelous things, things planned long ago.

—Isaiah 25:1 NIV

On a trip to Washington, D.C. in 2006, I decided to make the most of a three-day visit with some rather ambitious sightseeing. Blessed by unseasonably warm weather for late November, I was able to walk the city to view its imposing monuments. Pausing along the way, I read many carefully worded inscriptions. As if awakening from the coma of grief, I experienced a moment of divine illumination. My eyes and heart were opened to these eternal truths about the nature of God:

- God is ageless.
- God is timeless.
- God is unchanging.
- God is for all generations.

᠁ God is from everlasting to everlasting.

᠁ God is eternal.

᠁ God is faithful.

At the World War II memorial my hand traced slowly over a bronze relief depicting muddy soldiers fighting in the South Pacific, where my own father served for four years. In that moment of spiritual communion, the power of God's faithfulness, God's presence to all soldiers who have ever served, was very personal. God was in the foxhole with my father as he recited Psalm 23 for strength and courage. At the Vietnam memorial I found the name of a childhood friend who died in that war, remembering as though yesterday the heartbreak of his parents at the death of their only son. On that brilliant November day I grasped the reality that God has been there to comfort all who have ever grieved throughout all the ages of time. God is with all those who now serve. Then and there I began to emerge from the spiritual and emotional isolation of grief. I realized with absolute certainty that God is faithful. "Your love, O LORD, reaches to the heavens, your faithfulness to the skies" (Psalm 36:5 NIV).

When we attune our inmost heart to the reality of the present, we discern with gratitude every manifestation of God's faithfulness as we grieve:

᠁ God protects us. He watches over us as we live alone, perhaps for the first time in life.

᠁ God directs our worry and anxiety toward peace.

᠁ God is with us through the loneliness of grief.

᠁ God instructs us when we are required to make difficult decisions. We listen for God's wisdom in the quiet of our heart, "I bless the LORD who gives me counsel; in the night also my heart instructs me" (Psalm 16:7 NRSV).

- God blesses us with an extra measure of strength and forbearance. We ask ourselves in amazement, "How did I do that?" or "Did I really accomplish that?"
- God holds us in "the everlasting arms" (Deuteronomy 33:27 NIV).
- God lifts us when we are fallen.
- God strengthens us when we are weak.
- God encourages us when we are in despair.
- God wipes away our tears of sorrow.

God's faithfulness is evident in every aspect of our life.

- God provides for our needs.
- God uses others to minister to us in grief.
- God encourages us through the Holy Spirit.

"Know therefore that the LORD your God is God; He is the faithful God, keeping his covenant of love to a thousand generations of those who love him and keep his commands" (Deuteronomy 7:9 NIV). God is faithful. God is with us as we grieve.

Prayer

> I love the LORD, because he has heard
>> my voice and my supplications.
> Because he inclined his ear to me,
>> therefore I will call on him as long as I live.
> The snares of death encompassed me. . . .
>> I suffered distress and anguish.
> Then I called on the name of the LORD:
>> "O LORD, I pray, save my life!"
>
> —Psalm 116:1-4 NRSV

One of the most confusing aspects of grief is prayer. When our emotions are in turmoil, it is difficult to focus the mind and spirit to pray. We want to pray, yet we find no peaceful place within because our heart is consumed by anxiety and fear. After Leighton died my mind was a chaotic jumble of thoughts. My random prayers surely made little sense to God.

When we watch as a beloved husband or wife dies, we are spiritually debilitated by our own helplessness. In the urgent, quiet desperation that suggests impending grief, we are perhaps unable to pray. Our fervent, whispered pleas for healing and restoration are answered, but not with "yes." Through the heartache of death, we learn that the answer to prayer may be "wait" or "no." Because of the experience of death, our expectations of prayer may change. Yet we are assured that when we pray for comfort and strength, the answer to our prayer is always "yes." All prayers are answered.

- What did you pray for as you watched illness progress toward death, medicine insufficient to a deteriorating condition?
- What was the answer to your prayer?
- How did you react to the answer to your prayer—anger, disappointment, resentment, bewilderment?
- Do you believe that your prayers for healing were unanswered?

Why do we pray? We pray because God asks us to share our inmost being with the One who created you. We pray because God cares for us, because God is interested in every detail of our life. We pray not to enlighten God, but to discern the mind of God. Prayer draws us closer to God; it deepens our relationship with God. Prayer reminds us that we are dependent on God and not on ourselves. We pray because prayer alleviates spiritual weariness. God knows what we need before we pray; he answers even before we ask. God asks us that we lift our broken heart

- in prayer that is soul-searching and introspective
- in prayer that allows listening and meditation
- in prayer possible only within the silence of the heart
- in prayer for divine wisdom and insight

When pain is all-consuming, we may resist the impulse to pray. God understands; God carries our broken heart. Our prayer receptors seem broken. For a while it may seem that we cannot ask or receive answers to prayer. When grief is new, rife with our kaleidoscopic human emotion, every thought may be a form of prayer, an unbroken stream of consciousness conversation with God rather than a formal ritual at a predetermined time of day. This is one way we pray through our grief.

We surrender our will to God's will when we pray. When we acknowledge in prayer that we are not in control of life or death and pray in perfect trust "Thy will be done," we experience a humbling moment of grief. Praying "Thy will be done," is seeking, finding, and doing the will of God, not living in passive helplessness at the mercy of an inflictive, punitive God. In a sermon Leighton said:

> "Thy will be done" ought to be understood in the sense of perfect trust—a perfect trust in the perfect wisdom and perfect love of God. The will of God ought to be seen as that which is positive and affirmative and active in our life. When we pray "Thy will be done," we are not praying for weary resignation or forced acceptance. We are not praying to be taken out of a situation, but to be able to take it and conquer it, to defeat it and overcome it.[34]

A few months after Leighton died, I was at a gas station late one afternoon filling the car. I was still very tentative about life without him at my side. Even the most routine task challenged my very will to survive. A stranger approached me and introduced herself. She knew me, but I did not know her. My impulse was to withdraw in self-protection, yet her words touched the deepest place of my grief. She said that my name had been on her heart and that she was praying for me. It was a powerful moment. A complete stranger boldly dared to reach out and enfold me with spiritual care through prayer. As she turned away and left, I felt that I had been visited by an angel. Since that day there have been other experiences when God has used a stranger to minister to me. Have you been visited by an angel in grief? Has someone unexpectedly reached out, acknowledged your pain and sorrow, and given the gift of prayer to you?

Friends and family assure us that they are praying for us. If we feel unable to pray, we may allow the prayer of others to carry us for as long as we feel disconnected from God. It is not so much that we are unwilling to pray; rather when we grieve, the mind is in chaos, unable to offer more than the simplest expression of prayer. Even before we ask, we listen for the answer to our plea, "O LORD, I pray, save my life!" (Psalm 116:4 NRSV). The psalmist affirms that he answers: "Blessed be the LORD, for he has wondrously shown his steadfast love to me when I was beset as a city under siege. I had said in my alarm, 'I am driven far from your sight.' But you heard my supplications when I cried out to you for help" (Psalm 31:21-22 NRSV).

Praying for a husband or wife who has died is a religious tradition that is more Roman Catholic than Protestant. It is worth consideration, especially as a resolution to lingering guilt and regret. Yet if we find ourselves praying to our husband or wife as though we are praying to God, pause and remember that God is God; our spouse is not a co-God.

As I meditated in church one Sunday morning a few months after Leighton died, I was surprised to realize that I was praying for Leighton and his well-being. Prior to his death I never understood the purpose of praying for the dead. In my prayerful reverie there was spiritual resonance. And I received an answer: "He is alive; he is well." It was an answer that gave peace and comfort to my tortured soul. Prayer for our husband or wife is an act of communion; it is our spiritual acknowledgment that they live on, perfected in heaven.

Does our husband or wife pray for us? The Apostolic Church speaks of believers as saints, whether living or dead. Paul asked the saints to pray for him and imitate him. The Apostles Creed declares: "We believe in the communion of saints." If we pray for and with living saints in this life, we pray as well for and with those saints after mortal life has ended as part of the communion of saints.

Through prayer we grow spiritually; we are transformed and renewed. When we pray for others we abandon our self-involvement and acknowledge spiritual needs beyond the horizon of our own grief. When we are intentional about praying for family members, especially those affected by the loss of the person we are grieving, for our friends and co-workers, and for those in the world who are in need, we direct our thoughts and spirits toward the power of God's presence at work in our life.

The psalmists were faithful in prayer. Their impassioned cries to God were offered for others and about others, from the same place of personal loneliness and isolation that we experience in grief. We are blessed by the assurance of the psalms: "But God has surely listened and heard my voice in prayer" (Psalm 66:19 NIV). God listens. God is always there. God hears us when we pray. God answers prayer.

> *For those who walked with us, this is a prayer.*
> *For those who have gone ahead, this is a blessing.*
> *For those who have touched and tended us,*
> *Who lingered with us while they lived, this is a thanksgiving.*
> *For those who journey still with us in the shadows of awareness,*
> *In the crevices of memory, in the landscape of our dream,*
> *This is a benediction.*[35]

Comfort

Praise be to the God and Father of our Lord Jesus Christ, the Father of compassion and the God of all comfort, who comforts us in all our troubles, so that we can comfort those in any trouble with the comfort we ourselves receive from God.

—2 Corinthians 1:3-4 NIV

The word *comfort* is from the Latin *com fortis,* meaning "with strength." To be comforted is to be made strong. As we grieve, our comfort and strength are from the power and presence of the Holy Spirit. "And I will ask the Father, and he will give you another Comforter who will never leave you" (John 14:16 NLT).

A comforter is one who consoles. The One who can "comfort those in any trouble" is our Comforter. My father was my great comforter. He dabbed my cheeks with his large white handkerchief, gently murmuring, "Don't cry, Julie baby, don't cry." As he dried my tears and kissed away my hurt, he comforted me as only my father could. God is our great Comforter through the power of the Holy Spirit who never leaves us.

- Who is your comforter?
- Who penetrates your sadness with unspoken understanding?

❧ Who gives you emotional strength?

❧ Who inspires you with hope?

❧ Who is the safe person who responds to your grief with kind, thoughtful intentions?

In grief we forgive would-be comforters, those who try to console us with empty words or gestures. We expect others to understand what we are feeling, but it is not possible. We alone know the depth of our personal experience of grief. The truth is that no one can comfort us to our expectations; nor can we grieve to the expectations of another. Grief is not a job with a performance standard.

The nuances of comfort often qualify our grief. We experience the discomfort of mental and bodily distress as we struggle to adjust, adapt, and accept the death of our husband or wife. Childcare experts offer diverse opinions about whether to let an infant cry when it wakes at night because of some real or imagined discomfort or to allow the child time to soothe and self-comfort back to sleep. Certainly we hasten to comfort a helpless child, but how do we comfort ourselves through the discomfort of grief? As we explore and develop our instinct for self-comfort, we better understand that which truly comforts us in moments "beside the still waters." Much as a child finds solace in a worn blanket or favorite toy, discomfort is transformed as we better learn to comfort ourselves.

When we are overwhelmed by grief, we may be truly un-comfort-able, that is, unable to receive comfort from others or from God. For a while, it is not possible for us to be comforted by anyone or anything. Our deepest desire is not so much for comfort as it is for the return of life as it was. How do we open our heart to receive comfort? Through prayer in praise of God. In the Kaddish, a Jewish prayer said in memory of the dead, there is nothing about death. The power of its comfort reaches beyond death to extol the greatness of God in a memorial prayer in praise of God.

In a sermon on "Grief and Death," Leighton said, "Our lives are in the hands of a loving, caring, merciful God. God cares about us. God cares about us in our moments of grief; God cares about us in our moments of death. I can commend to you a God who loves you, cares about you, who will hold you in his arms if you will let Him."[36] As he spoke, he poured the power and passion of his faith into the word "cares." Neither he nor I could know at that time that his words of grace and comfort were meant for me.

God's comfort affirms the reality of the unseen as the very definition of faith: "Now faith is being sure of what we hope for and certain of what we do not see" (Hebrews 11:1 NIV).

Certainly we cannot prove it, but each of us has perhaps had evidence of the abiding spiritual presence of our husband or wife after death that affirms the reality of the unseen. Perhaps something occurred that you know without question was an unmistakable sign or signal that you alone would understand. Its power and force affirmed to you the real, eternal presence of your husband or wife. I sat in church one day celebrating in community the rite of infant baptism. When asked to name their tiny daughter, the proud parents said "Leighton." In the moment that the name was spoken, he was there with me. His presence was so powerful it took my breath away. He was everywhere—beside me and within me. I knew then as I know now that he lives eternally in the reality of the unseen.

The reality of the unseen comforts us. God explains more of the mystery of our trust in 1 Corinthians 13:12: "For now we see only a reflection as in a mirror; then we shall see face to face. Now I know in part; then I shall know fully, even as I am fully known" (NIV). For now, the reality of the unseen is a mystery. It is God's mystery of life and death. We cannot see it, but we experience God's comfort in the reality of eternal life, which is the very promise of faith.

As Leighton lay dying, the only world event that captured his attention was the death of President Ronald Reagan. We sat together watching the solemn funeral, silently denying that this ritual would affect us both imminently. I was profoundly moved by the anthem, which was the familiar JERUSALEM hymn tune by C. H. H. Parry set to words by Horatius Bonar. Less than one month later the National Cathedral arrangement was procured for use at Leighton's funeral service. The words would become my personal mantra of comfort through grief.

> *O love of God, how strong and true!*
> *Eternal, and yet ever new;*
> *Uncomprehended and unbought,*
> *Beyond all knowledge and all thought.*
> *O love of God, how deep and great!*
> *Far deeper than man's deepest hate;*
> *Self-fed, self-kindled, like the light,*
> *Changeless, eternal, infinite.*
> *O heavenly love, how precious still,*
> *In days of weariness and ill,*
> *In nights of pain and helplessness,*
> *To heal, to comfort, and to bless!*
> *O wide embracing, wondrous love!*
> *We read thee in the sky above,*
> *We read thee in the earth below,*
> *In seas that swell, and streams that flow.*
> *We read thee best in Him Who came*
> *To bear for us the cross of shame;*
> *Sent by the Father from on high,*
> *Our life to live, our death to die.*

We read thy power to bless and save
E'en in the darkness of the grave;
Still more in resurrection light,
We read the fullness of thy might.
O love of God, our shield and stay
Through all the perils of our way!
Eternal love, in thee we rest
Forever safe, forever blest.

—Horatius Bonar (1808–1889), "The Love of God"[37]

How Long Does Grief Last?

Very truly I tell you, you will weep and mourn while the world re-joices. You will grieve, but your grief will turn to joy.

—John 16:20 NIV

How long does grief last? The answer to this question of grief is an ongoing personal discovery as our individual issues of grief are confronted and resolved. Grief does not follow the calendar; it is not a straight-line experience. Grief comes and it goes; it ebbs and it flows. Imperceptibly, we learn to live alongside grief, but grief usually lasts longer than most of us expect, for grief will not be rushed. Poet Henry Taylor wrote, "He that lacks time to mourn, lacks time to mend."[38]

The infrastructure of life consists of both beginning and end. As human beings we want to control the "when" of both the beginning and the end of most things in life. Because grief is our emotional reaction to the event of death, its onset and end are unique and individual. Each person starts at a different point. For example, grief may have had its beginning as an undertow that swelled through stages of illness, crashing onto the shore of our well-ordered life with its full force and effect as the end of life nears. Whatever the circumstance, when and how grief begins may affect how long grief lasts.

Because grief defies an exact moment, our instinct may be to ignore it rather than enter into it. Some choose simply to hang on mindlessly until grief is over. In fact, we do not enter into grief. Grief enters into us. We move from "Why did this happen?" to "How will I go on?" We progress from disbelief and shock to the reality of life without our husband or wife. As the forward dynamic of life gradually redirects our grief, we become more immersed in the positive, life-sustaining memories of our marriage than the unalterable fact of death.

For some, it may take several years to work through profound loss and grief—the kind of "no end in sight" emotional turmoil that requires the insight of a professional. For others, there may be a defining moment such as remarriage that clearly signifies the end of grief. Because our emotions do not conform to life's infrastructure, the end of grief is personal. How long grief lasts is an intimate process of self-determination. We grieve as long as we grieve.

Each year on the anniversary of September 11, 2001, the enduring grief of those whose loved ones died on that fateful day is once again compelling. A few years ago on the sixth anniversary, a reporter for the *New York Times* wrote an article that implied that "by now," six years after the event that changed all of life forever, survivors should "be over" the worst of their grief and should be willing to scale down the annual public commemoration of that horrible day. In the article, the reporter quoted a nursing supervisor who used the term "shelf life" in reference to the survivors' grief.[39] This rather callous journalistic suggestion, rife with implied judgment, questions the validity and duration of individual grief. The survivors of 9/11 will always grieve. The premise that there is a "shelf life" for grief denies the most solemn and personal aspect of death: *we must grieve in order to live.*

Is there a "shelf life" for grief? For anyone who has experienced death in the first person, the answer is assuredly "no." Figuratively you may box up and shelve your unresolved issues for a while. But eventually you may revisit them, from the improved perspective of time. When you do, you look through what's there and touch it again. Perhaps you hold it close and reexamine it. You may decide to let it go or hold on to it and put it back on the shelf. Or you may decide to file it, put it in another box of odds and ends, shred it, scrap it, or put it on a figurative bonfire and burn it. This is the only real "shelf life" that pertains to grief. And unlike well-marked packages at a supermarket, there is no expiration date on grief.

Although it is not usually so, in some instances grief may last a lifetime. Queen Victoria made a public and private career of long-term grief as the eternal widow of Windsor. In 1840 Victoria married her mother's nephew Albert who, as husband and prince consort, was the center of her life. He was her confidant, friend, and advisor. They were married twenty-one years and had nine children. When he died in 1861, Victoria was only forty-two.

The Queen's grief was profound. She did not appear in public for three years and wore mourning clothes for over ten years. Her subjects thought her response to death exaggerated, shocking, and abnormal because she would not be moved from her grief. An entire nation expected her to abandon grief and "get on with life."

When she emerged from her self-imposed seclusion, Victoria felt her return to public life was a betrayal of her husband. She suffered from chronic, prolonged depression, physically crippled by grief. Yet she lived another forty years as Queen and Empress of a vast empire. She never recovered; she grieved without apology or explanation until she died. Victoria grieved for a lifetime; there was no "shelf life" to her grief.

"Very truly I tell you the truth, you will weep and mourn while the world rejoices. You will grieve, but your grief will turn to joy" (John 16:20 NIV). Though we have no instructions on how long our grief lasts or how long we should grieve, our assurance is that grief will turn to joy.

- Grief turns to joy when life blossoms in unexpected ways that bring renewal and hope for the future.
- Grief turns to joy in moments that celebrate the life and love of our husband or wife.
- Grief turns to joy with the birth of a child or grandchild.
- Grief turns to joy with a new companion for the rest of life's journey.
- Grief will turn to joy when at last we are reunited with the one we have grieved in life and in death.

So, how long does grief last? Grief lasts as long as it lasts.

Solitude

In quietness and confidence shall be your strength.

—*Isaiah 30:15 NKJV*

Solitude is aloneness without loneliness. It is the quiet within peace as we befriend our aloneness. Solitude is the peace "that surpasses all understanding" (Philippians 4:7 NRSV). Solitude is the incubator of the listening heart; it is the stillness within self-understanding and renewed strength.

The quiet heart waits in yearning patience
To find the Mind of God.
    —*John Ness Beck, "The Quiet Heart"*[40]

Solitude and loneliness are not the same. Loneliness suggests that we are not sufficiently at home within our self to benefit from emotionally productive time alone. According to Henri Nouwen, "[Solitude] means daring to stand in God's presence...alone in God's company."[41] Alone means completeness within our own being—*all +one*. The late psychologist, writer, and television host Eda LeShan wrote, "When we cannot bear to be alone, it means we do not properly value the only companion we will have from birth to death—ourselves."[42]

Solitude is being alone without being lonely. Solitude is comfort within the confines of our own being. Protestant theologian Paul Tillich wrote: "Language...has created the word 'loneliness' to express the pain of being alone. And it has created the word 'solitude' to express the glory of being alone....Loneliness can be conquered only by those who can bear solitude."[43]

Sleep is nature's way of ensuring solitude. The body and mind are restored through the power of silence. Statesman William Penn observed, "True silence is the rest of the mind, and is to the spirit what sleep is to the body, nourishment and refreshment."[44] God is with us in silence and in solitude.

Where is solitude amid the white noise of the world in which we live? Solitude is both in aloneness and in the presence of others. Solitude is a state, a destination for our spirit that is intermittent and unpredictable. Like Thoreau at Walden Pond, solitude may be an intentional choice of place or time that nourishes the soul and welcomes us into communion with ourselves.

Solitude inspires the courage of our own self-awareness as we adjust to the vicissitudes of grief. In solitude our inner voice speaks. This is the voice of both our conscious and subconscious minds; it always requires solitude to be heard and understood. Our inner voice is the steady participant in our internal, circular conversation of the mind. In grief, random thoughts constantly swirl through our mind as memories bang around in our head and heart. When we consciously release them, or better yet discard them, space is made for others to bubble up in their place. If we listen, our own inner voice clearly articulates the deep, unfathomed emotions well beyond our conscious recognition. At that place of oneness within ourselves, from the depth of the subconscious our inmost feelings illuminate our grief.

Well beyond the suggestions of our own inner voice, in solitude our eternal spirit is able to focus on the voice of God speaking to us through the Holy Spirit. Scottish theologian William Barclay wrote, "God is not silent, and again and again, when the strain of life is too much for us, and the effort of his way is beyond our human resources, if we listen we will hear him speak, and we will go on with his strength surging through our frame. Our trouble is not that God does not speak, but that we do not listen."[45]

Solitude is not withdrawal from life in monastic silence or antisocial behavior. Solitude is not a way of life; rather it is a way of finding life. In his poem "The Church Porch," seventeenth-century poet George Herbert urged, "By all means find some time to be alone. Salute thyself and see what thy soul wears."[46] Solitude is an innate need, especially as we grieve. After the death of our husband or wife, we are blessed by the space and quiet of solitude to do the work of grief. As Henri Nouwen noted, "Solitude, where we absent ourselves from the myriad voices that tell us otherwise, helps us hear again that voice of love."[47]

The soul-searching questions of grief are resolved through the enrichment of solitude with answers found only in the quiet of the heart.

- Why did my husband or wife die?
- Why am I still alive?
- What am I alive for?
- Do my children still need parenting?
- Am I here to influence and support my grandchildren?
- Am I here to serve others in the world?
- What is the purpose of my life?
- What is the meaning of my life?
- How do I find my way in life?

According to Roman Marcus Aurelius, "Nowhere can man find a quieter or more untroubled retreat than in his own soul."[48] Solitude reconciles our experience of death to life. The soul at one with solitude invites the power of the Holy Spirit to comfort and restore, "In quietness and confidence shall be your strength" (Isaiah 30:15 NKJV).

Adjustment

⟨ ～～～～～ ⟩

But this one thing I do: forgetting what lies behind and straining forward to what lies ahead, I press on toward the goal for the prize of the heavenly call of God in Christ Jesus.

—*Philippians 3:13-14 NRSV*

Adjustment often refers to actions accomplished in a single, deft move.

- ❧ We adjust the temperature in our home for a comfortable living environment.
- ❧ We adjust the setting on the radio or television to assure optimal quality for entertainment pleasure.
- ❧ We adjust the rear and side view mirrors of the car before driving.
- ❧ We adjust our belt when we overeat.
- ❧ We adjust the fit of our clothes when we gain or lose weight.
- ❧ We make a claim when property is damaged; an adjuster estimates the cost of repair.
- ❧ We pay taxes on our adjusted gross income.
- ❧ We receive a cost-of-living adjustment.

Life is about constant, subtle adjustment. Intuitively we conform to circumstance. God has given us the ability to assess and adapt; we are innately equipped to adjust. Adjustment assumes monumental proportions when we grieve. According to British biologist and philosopher John Mason Tyler, "Life is the continual adjustment of internal relations to external relations or conditions."[49] Adjustment is the gradual process that moves us toward acceptance of loss.

Fast-forward adjustment begins with physical debilitation, a terminal diagnosis, or a fatal accident. At once it is necessary to adjust from our familiar partnership to a life bereft of its structure and support, and then again to life as it is. Adjustment is suddenly an intuitive necessity rather than a conscious act.

For a while we hold on desperately to all that has passed away from our life. Our struggle to adjust may be a stubborn defense of the past, a reluctance to embrace the present, or obstruction of hope for the future. What makes adjustment so difficult? American philosopher Eric Hoffer affirms, "We have to adjust ourselves, and every new adjustment is a crisis in self-esteem."[50] We have spent all or part of our adult life in the relationship of marriage as part of a couple physically dissolved by the event of death.

- We adjust to the absence of our husband or wife.
- We adjust to a home that seems suddenly silent and empty.
- We adjust to the loss of a listening ear; we turn to speak and no one is there. There is a void where we have listened and been heard.
- We adjust to the loss of the love, care, and daily concern of our spouse.
- We adjust to physical aloneness when life has been so inextricably entwined with another.
- We adjust to the reality of daily life.
- We eat alone.

- We provide for ourselves.

- We are our own caregiver.

- We learn new modalities of independence.

- We learn how to function without our husband or wife.

- We adjust our self-perception as we go into the world alone.

- We learn more about confidence, courage, and self-affirmation.

- We learn to individuate into life without our spouse.

- We adjust to the role of sole parent to our children, fulfilling the role of mother and father, grandmother and grandfather.

- We endow future generations with our shared legacy of love and generosity.

- We adjust to personal management of our finances, health, and social interaction with others.

Adjustment is stretching; it is the discovery that we are more resilient than we imagine. Slowly we realize that we can let go and hold on at the same time in one seamless emotional stand. "Everything old has passed away; see, everything has become new!" (2 Corinthians 5:17 NRSV). As we adjust, we let go of the physical life that once was and will never be again, but we do not forget. What lies behind is our history; it is part of who we will yet become. The past informs the rest of the life that we have been given to live. We cherish the unforgettable; we build on the past and hold on to all that gives value and worth to life, conformed to the reality of the present.

In his book *The Inner Voice of Love: A Journey Through Anguish to Freedom*, Henri Nouwen wrote, "You will see that you are no longer there: the past is gone, the pain has left you, you no longer have to go back and relive it, you no longer depend on your past to identify yourself.... From the perspective of the life you now live and the distance you now have, your past does not loom over you. It has lost its weight and can be remembered as God's way of making you more compassionate and understanding toward others."[51]

"But this one thing I do: forgetting what lies behind and straining forward to what lies ahead, I press on toward the goal for the prize" (Philippians 3:13 NRSV). Within adjustment lies the promise that there is yet life for which to strain forward, that something does lie ahead. There is a goal; there is a prize with notes of joy and possibility. God has a purpose for each of us while we yet have breath on this earth. Though it may seem so for a while, we did not die physically with our husband or wife.

Going through grief and moving forward in grief is the slow work of constant adjustment. As we adjust we reanimate not only to life, but also to our own fullness of life. Like a thoroughbred race horse running full out for the finish line, we press on toward the goal for the prize, straining forward toward new life. When we relax into the future with faith, we claim the prize of the high calling of God for life today, tomorrow, and evermore.

Acceptance

We know that in everything God works for good with those who love him, who are called according to his purpose.

—Romans 8:28 RSV

As we journey through grief, we follow the path through the valley of the shadow of death. First we descend its depths; then, slowly but surely, we ascend, always moving toward acceptance. Yet on the way to acceptance we perhaps pause for a moment to take a final backward glance. We remember the dark sadness and sorrow and the emotional turmoil of compelling grief that once held us captive. On the other side of grief, at last we see clearly where we have been and what we have been through. We realize with gratitude that acceptance has been the consistent trajectory of grief. We complete the journey because we have dared to travel this lonely, deserted road of the heart.

Acceptance is slow metamorphosis; it is the emotional maturing of our adjustment to life as it is becoming. When adjustment becomes the norm, we move resolutely towards acceptance. Reluctantly we accept that our spouse is physically gone and acknowledge this as permanent. We understand what happened and that the outcome cannot be changed. Though we do not like it, we accept it. As we have done so faithfully with grief, we work at acceptance. Perhaps we are able to time-date a moment of acceptance, or acceptance simply occurs. We near acceptance when we at last acknowledge that we are no longer actively grieving.

If we allow grief to defeat our spirit, acceptance may be dull resignation. Grace, courage and wisdom are the hallmarks of acceptance. Protestant theologian Reinhold Niebuhr amplified the well-known serenity prayer of Saint Francis of Assisi:

> God, give us grace to accept with serenity
> the things that cannot be changed,
> courage to change the things
> that should be changed,
> and the wisdom to distinguish
> the one from the other.[52]

In acceptance we transcend physical loss and embrace the spirit of our spouse's life and love that remains with us always. In *Transcending Loss*, psychotherapist and grief counselor Ashley Davis Prend states, "Death doesn't end the relationship, it simply forges a new type of relationship—one based not on physical presence but on memory, spirit, and love."[53] As adjustment slowly shifts to acceptance, the cold reality of absence is eased by the certainty of enduring love. "Love and faithfulness meet together; righteousness and peace kiss each other. Faithfulness springs forth from the earth, and righteousness looks down from heaven" (Psalm 85:10-11 NIV). One widow observes, "My grief is more than just a collection of memories. It helps me define who I am now; it gives shape and substance to the relationship I have with my loved one. For without my grief, I could not have a connection to him."

The whispered spiritual presence of our husband or wife surrounds us each day, encouraging us to live on and share our legacy of love. The core of acceptance is indwelling—the indwelling of the love of your husband or wife and the indwelling of the love of God. Author Molly Fumia reflects, "I first grieve by allowing you to take over my heart, struggling with your presence, sparring with the unspeakable idea that you are gone. My heart is occupied by memory and finality. I next grieve by making room in that captive heart for myself. We must meet there one more time, you and I, to bind together in a common presence that is edgeless, endless. In that awareness, I can feel the uprising of an old ally. The self I still am continues, side by side in the universe, with the self you will always be, but insists I reclaim my heart as my own."[54]

"We know that in everything God works for good with those who love him, who are called according to his purpose" (Romans 8:28 RSV). As survivors we wonder how the death of our husband or wife can possibly be for good in our life. The case for acceptance lies with the prepositions: *in* everything God works *for* good, *with* those who love him.

- Our loss and sorrow are not ordained by God. Rather, God meets us at our place of brokenness; God is there *in* everything.
- God uses grief to teach us more of God's faithfulness and steadfast love. God works *for* good, using that which has changed our life to promote a deeper, more profound faith.
- God works *with* us because we are called according to God's purpose, that is, because we have faith in God's plan for our life. God leads us and works *with* us to shape a life of meaning and purpose.

Everything new is an outward reflection of our growing acceptance. If we buy sheets, decide on a new car, take a trip, or move our place of residence, we affirm acceptance of life as it is. Within the balance of loss and acceptance, equalized by a more mature faith, our heart urges us to live forward.

Finally, acceptance is victory. It is the strength and power of an unconquerable soul. As clouds of doubt and fear slowly drift away, we stand at last in the radiance of full sunlight, assured from within that there is life beyond grief because there is life after death.

Happiness

"Blessed are those who mourn, for they will be comforted."
—Matthew 5:4 NRSV

As grief progresses beyond the pain of loss and loneliness, we ask ourselves, "Will I ever be happy again?" We perhaps answer, "I might be happy again if only something would change so that everything would be better," a thought that denies the reality of grief.

"Blessed are those who mourn, for they will be comforted" (NRSV), is the fourth beatitude or "declaration of blessedness" from the Sermon on the Mount (see Matthew 5:1-12). This counterintuitive promise assures us that because we mourn, we will be *blessed*—or, in the Greek, *happy*. The connection between blessedness and happiness lies within the word "beatitude," from the Latin *beatitude*, meaning "state of blessedness," from *beatus*, meaning "happy, blessed," and from *beare*, meaning "to make happy."

We struggle to reconcile blessedness and mourning, happiness and grief. We may look at it this way: Because we mourn, we are comforted; when we are comforted, then we are, in turn, blessed. Because mourning is the expression of our inmost sorrow, grief insists that we mourn before we are blessed with authentic comfort and happiness.

What is happiness? The root of the word happiness is *hap*, which means "fortune or chance."[55] It is found in words of both positive and negative connotation: happening, mishap, haphazard, and happenstance. The unstated meaning of happiness is that chance or fortune determine our state of being—that we are not entirely in charge of our own happiness.

For some, happiness is a way of life. Those with a sunny disposition often are sustained through grief by a greater sense of hope and optimism than those who are by nature more introverted or reserved.

In her best-selling book *Eat, Pray, Love*, Elizabeth Gilbert wrote this:

> People universally tend to think that happiness is a stroke of luck or something that will maybe descend upon you like fine weather if you're fortunate enough. But that's not how happiness works. Happiness is the consequence of personal effort. You fight for it, strive for it, insist upon it, and sometimes even travel around the world looking for it. You have to participate relentlessly in the manifestations of your own blessings. And once you have achieved a state of happiness, you must never become lax about maintaining it, you must make a mighty effort to keep swimming upward into that happiness forever, to stay afloat on top of it."[56]

Happiness, then, is the reward. It is the result of something we have already done: we have mourned. Happiness comes to us by indirection: "Blessed are those who mourn, for they will be comforted" (Matthew 5:4 NRSV).

Happiness is the by-product of our inner stability rather than our outward security. In grief we explore and discover, perhaps for the first time in life, the depth of our own inner stability. Although our sense of well-being is affected by death, we are not wholly at the mercy of happenstance or outward circumstance. Rather, happiness is the triumph of our inner stability over our outward security.

Often quiet desperation, loneliness, and emotional misery drive the pursuit of superficial happiness. The media suggests every day what will make us happy. Family and friends want to reconstruct our happiness according to *their* idea of our well-being. The truth is that happiness comes only from within. Happiness is an inside story. It begins where we are; it happens from within the heart.

- ❧ What makes me happy?
- ❧ When am I happy?
- ❧ Do I have the inner resources to live a life of sustained happiness?

Seventeenth-century English essayist Joseph Addison wrote, "Three grand essentials to happiness in this life are something to do, something to love, and something to hope for."[57] As life unfolds, happiness may be more about cause and effect. Though we are still lonely from time to time, at last we grow accustomed to being alone. Life slowly flourishes with renewed energy that begins to feel like happiness. If what we experience is not exactly happiness, then perhaps it is a kind of quiet contentment that honors the memory of a joyful marriage.

A life of service is the secret of happiness. Speaking with a group of children, Albert Schweitzer is reported to have said, "I don't know what your destiny will be, but one thing I know, the only ones among you who will be really happy are those who have sought and found a way to serve."[58] The happy person is one who comforts having been comforted, one who loves having been loved, one who finds life in giving it away. In giving we receive; in selflessness, we find. This is authentic happiness.

Spiritual happiness is only a small step away from joy, the ultimate quest of our grief journey. Joy is the balance of peace and hope that resides deep within our human heart. "Blessed are those who mourn, for they will be comforted" (Matthew 5:4 NRSV).

Healing

⁓

He heals the brokenhearted, and binds up their wounds.

—Psalm 147:3 NRSV

Is there healing in grief? Is there healing from grief? The best analogy is the human body. Physical injury causes a wound of finite, reparable damage that can be treated with expectation of healing. Death wounds the human soul and spirit; it causes us to grieve. For some the wound is immeasurable—so deep that healing seems impossible. For others, the wound is less severe. The greater the love for our husband or wife, the larger and deeper our wound.

Like any physical injury, the wound of grief must be taken seriously. Honest, accurate assessment facilitates its treatment, both mentally and spiritually. For many, the wound is caused by slow leave-taking after months or years of chronic illness. For others, death is a tragic, gaping wound in need of immediate, acute care. Many unresolved circumstances may compound our trauma:

⁓ The unexpected onset of disease when our husband or wife seemed otherwise healthy.

- The rapid demise of our husband or wife.
- The affliction, pain, and suffering caused by a disease that could not be treated or conquered.
- The loss of control in life.

As with the body, we treat our wound with constructive pain relievers:

- Work
- Church
- Community service/voluntarism
- Hobby
- Recreation
- Travel
- Children, grandchildren, friends

In moments of acute woundedness we may try to anesthetize our pain with easy remedies (alcohol, food, medication), yet we know this does not work. Quick cures seldom last. God is the one true source of reconstructive relief from the pain of grief, "He heals the brokenhearted and binds up their wounds" (Psalm 147:3 NRSV).

Relentless, unremitting grief is an infection that invades the wound of our soul. When grief permanently overwhelms us, it destroys our very will to live. When our grief is tenacious, spiritual healing begins only when we affirm that we want to be made well and that we want our journey through grief to be over. In her book *Safe Passage*, Molly Fumia writes, "Healing is not a wish that can be granted by someone else. It is a well within us that we alone can tap. It is a desire that we allow for, in our own time, by our own choosing."[59]

When we are injured, wound dressings are carefully applied to our physical body to promote healing and protect the point of invasion from germs. Similarly, in grief we slap a figurative bandage on our wound, not so much to promote healing, but to protect ourselves from additional hurt and pain. Because we sense that others do not want to see the gaping hole in our spirit—the imperfect part of our life that is grief—we cover it up with a self-styled emotional wound dressing.

- For friends our bandage is decorated with ridiculous yellow happy faces that considerately distract them from our grief.
- For children and grandchildren, our bandage is perhaps a "tough strip," designed to be both protective and impervious.
- For others, we perhaps disguise our woundedness with a clear bandage that conceals our hurt yet does not make our injury truly invisible.
- If we are indifferent to appearance, perhaps we apply a clumsy bandage of gauze and tape.
- Or perhaps we abandon convention altogether and grieve openly, our gaping emotional wound uncovered, visible for all to see.

Assuming that there is some improvement, we risk the smart of momentary pain when we rip our bandage from the skin—ouch! Likewise, when our wound is reopened and exposed by inevitable remembrance days, we are reminded that we are still vulnerable to pain. We examine the damage and discern that our wound is healing from the inside. We realize that revisiting a painful moment is not a complete re-injury; rather, it is a brief uncovering that requires only the fresh bandage of a new day.

We wonder how long it takes to heal and when we will know we are healed. It is unclear how we will know that we are healed. The answer is that healing is not linear. There is no time line or prescribed cure date for grief. Healing is the gradual process of becoming whole or sound. When we at last take off our protective bandage and find that we are well, we see that we are healed both from within and without.

Spiritual and emotional healing from grief is perhaps better described as recovery. To recover is "to convalesce, forge ahead, get better, grow, overcome, pull through, recuperate, restore, start anew, turn a corner."[60] If you are finding satisfaction in life with renewed self-confidence, you are recovering. If you have heard yourself say, whether silently or aloud, "I am better," "I want to live," "Life is good," or other self-talk that is affirmative and positive, this is a sure indication of recovery from grief.

As with the physical body, there is a scar forever in our soul to remind us of our grief. It is at first red and tender, then slowly fades until it is almost invisible. It is a medical fact that scar tissue becomes the strongest part of our body. As our spirit and heart slowly mend, we become strongest in our broken places—within the very fiber of our soul. Our scar, the spiritual and emotional reminder of our most acute pain, is now part of who we are. Our scar affirms the best part of our own immortality, our soul. Though we are wounded by the death of a beloved husband or wife, we are healed by God's triumphant adequacy: "He heals the brokenhearted and binds up their wounds" (Psalm 147:3 NRSV).

Hope

But this I call to mind, and therefore I have hope: The steadfast love of the LORD never ceases; his mercies never come to an end; they are new every morning; great is your faithfulness. "The LORD is my portion," says my soul, "therefore I will hope in him."

—Lamentations 3:21-24 ESV

Hope is the teaser of headlines. We read the paper expecting good news, yet often the story belies real hope. Without hope life is bland and uninspired. Hope is the salt that flavors our life; hope is the seasoning that adds spice to our expectation of life.

Hopelessness is the dark underside of grief. Grief assails our hope; without hope we despair. When we despair, we drift into cynical acceptance or defeated resignation. "Why are you in despair, O my soul? And why are you disturbed within me? Hope in God, for I shall again praise Him, the help of my countenance and my God" (Psalm 43:5 NASB). Hope leaves no room for despair.

Hope is more than an emotion. We hope because we are divinely created human beings. No matter how dire the circumstances of impending death, we continue to hope. Even when we are confronted with a hopeless situation, we hope because we cannot imagine death, or how life will be without our husband or wife. The innate human instinct that denies our very mortality is always informed by hope. Irish writer and playwright Oliver Goldsmith wrote, "Hope, like a gleaming taper's light, adorns and cheers our way. And still, as darker grows the night, emits a brighter ray."[61]

Although hope does not erase the reality of death, grief need not be a place of emotional surrender and existential catastrophe. Grief can be the most honest, whole, and faithful place we can possibly stand and find hope. For a while hope may feel more like tentative renewal than exuberant life. This place of emotional and spiritual suspended animation may feel for a while rather tepid and lukewarm. Hope, then, is also a quiet phase—a time of readying, resting, and regrouping after the long journey through grief. This is the time to breathe, relax, rest, and live—one day at a time.

Hope is the conviction that the desirable is obtainable and that events will turn out for the best. Hope implies perseverance, the belief that a positive outcome is possible even in the face of evidence to the contrary. Hope is based in reality:

- Hope is not naïve optimism.
- Hope is not wishful thinking.
- Hope is not a positive attitude.
- Hope is not a passive wish or dream.

With its formidable power to transform us, hope is our fear defeated. The hope of grief is confidence in the divine plan of a loving, caring God—the author of all hope. "Now hope that is seen is not hope. For who hopes for what is seen? But if we hope for what we do not see, we wait for it with patience" (Romans 8:24b-25 NRSV). In the will to hope we find strength to live and courage to die.

We are to "rejoice in hope, be patient in suffering, persevere in prayer" (Romans 12:12 NRSV). The most active form of our hope is expressed in prayer. "The widow who is really in need and left all alone puts her hope in God and continues night and day to pray and to ask God for help" (1 Timothy 5:5 NIV). In prayer we entrust the most fervent desires of our heart to God because we desire restoration to life. We hope because we have faith.

Hope, then, is sacred evidence of expectancy, patience, trust, and faith. "In this life we have three great lasting qualities—faith, hope and love. But the greatest of them is love" (1 Corinthians 13:13 JBP). Hope stands in the middle—its bookends are faith and love. What God has done through faith, hope, and love illuminates what God will do. Hope does not rely on our own aspirations but upon God. We hope for the future because the future belongs to God. "And hope does not disappoint us, because God has poured out his love into our hearts by the Holy Spirit, whom he has given us" (Romans 5:5 NIV). In bold declaration of faith we affirm that hope does not disappoint us, for in God, the best is yet to be.

> *Be strong and take heart, all you who hope in the LORD.*
> *—Psalm 31:24 NIV*

> *May the God of hope fill you with all joy and peace as you trust in him,*
> *so that you may overflow with hope by the power of the Holy Spirit.*
> *—Romans 15:13 NIV*

> *May your unfailing love rest upon us, LORD, even as we put our hope*
> *in you.*
> *—Psalm 33:22 NIV*

Reconstruction

Unless the LORD builds the house, those who build it labor in vain.
—Psalm 127:1 NRSV

A contractor or building design specialist perhaps would agree that it is easier to build a new structure than remodel an old one. Buildings and homes usually decline into functional obsolescence after a period of use if not updated or modernized to current standards.

Construction teems with positive energy. The unmistakable bouquet of the smell of fresh sawdust suggests the promise of a completed project, sparkling new at the end. Reconstruction honors the existence of something worth salvaging, of remaining life within a structure, regardless of its condition. In grief, that structure is our very life; our task is building anew, constructing again.

Remodeling to accommodate life without our husband or wife is our daily work of grief. As we move forward, our personal reconstruction project perhaps stimulates both our mind and heart, stretching us to contemplate the practically endless possibilities for new life.

❧ How do we reconstruct a life of meaning and purpose?

❧ How do we reconstitute our daily existence without our spouse?

❧ How do we remodel from within without the luxury of creating an entirely new personal structure?

The most essential part of any structure is a sound foundation. "The rain came down, the streams rose, and the winds blew and beat against that house; yet it did not fall, because it had its foundation on the rock" (Matthew 7:25 NIV). When our life is deconstructed by death, our structure seems at times near total collapse. Tremors of loss and sorrow quake the bedrock of our soul. Yet we stand—our footing secured by the unshakeable foundation that never fails. We build our life on the rock, which is the faithful, steadfast love of God. "Unless the LORD builds the house, those who build it labor in vain" (Psalm 127:1 NRSV). The sacred ground on which we rebuild cannot be destroyed. It is indestructible.

My father was in the commercial construction business for thirty-five years, the proud owner of a sole proprietorship dedicated to excellence. On a hot July day, I sat in my car and wept openly as I watched a large, impressively destructive bulldozer knock down his former office building in the name of progress. The physical symbol of his labor and investment over a professional lifetime was reduced to a pile of twisted rubble in a matter of minutes, the remains an odd mixture of dusty, unusable material. Similarly, when our husband or wife dies the ordered structure of a lifetime together is razed, destroyed with a single final breath.

After my father died I found Luke 14:28-30 marked in his Bible, noted in his precise engineer's handwriting as the Estimator's Verse: "For which of you, desiring to build a tower, does not first sit down and count the cost, whether he has enough to complete it? Otherwise, when he has laid a foundation, and is not able to finish, all who see it begin to mock him, saying, 'This man began to build, and was not able to finish'" (ESV).

Throughout the course of grief we may, likewise, stop, sit down, and count the cost of whether we want to rebuild our life.

- Do we want to expend the effort for an unknown future?
- Do we have the stamina, discipline, and will to complete our personal reconstruction?
- Are we influenced by the judgment and opinion of others as we seek to rebuild a new life of our own design?
- Do we have the determination to work at our own pace, with completion at some unknown time, sooner or later?

Some basic principles of construction apply to our rebuilding project:

- There is a plan to follow.
  - There is a design, conventional or free-form.
  - There are construction steps that must occur in sequential order.
  - As structure takes form, the plan may change. A newspaper reports that a major urban cultural project was changed more than fifty times. Structure may be altered by circumstance—remarriage, infirmity, death. When that happens, we change the plan. We try again and build forward. As we reconfigure our life, we reorder the daily into a place that feels like emotional home—a place we want to live.

- Construction is hard work.
  - A construction worker is usually covered in dirt at the end of a day's labor. The hard work of construction requires physical strength, aptitude, skill, and commitment to complete the job with skilled proficiency. Likewise, grief is hard work. Because

we are unpracticed, the labor of reconstruction may seem emotionally and physically exhausting. Gradually we build, placing one block of experience carefully upon the last. As our self-renewal project takes form and shape, an improved structure emerges from the building materials of grief.

~ Construction is hand-work.

- In construction, heavy machinery is used for clearing, digging, and hoisting. Materials are manufactured and prepared by industry; labor-saving tools are used to expedite efficiency. But hands guide the power saw, the nail gun, the riveter, the end of the girder as one nail, one bolt, one rivet, one girder at a time is affixed and fastened into place. Construction is essentially the hand-work of human beings, the life force of creative energy that elevates building from a science to art. If this were not so, complex robotics alone might be used to erect otherwise soulless structures.

- The hands of a construction laborer show the wear and tear of hard use. Seldom is a good worker without a bruise under the fingernail, a silent badge of hand-work. Similarly, in grief we are bruised under our emotional exterior. We may wear figurative gloves to protect ourselves from contact, commitment, or the inevitable march of progress through our life. As with a physical bruise, the injury of grief usually resolves over time.

- At last we roll up our sleeves and do the hands-on work of rebuilding our structure as personal growth propels our project forward. The work is messy, the work is dirty, but construction is always productive.

◦ Construction requires tools.

- My father believed that a well-equipped tool box was an essential life accessory. He knew that the right tool was critical to the success of any job. In the hand-work of reconstruction, we may use symbolic tools to alter the structure of our life: we hammer, unscrew, saw off, pull out, level, and realign. We modify in order to "start fresh" in a recreated life.

◦ Reconstruction is the work of self-nurture.

- As we remodel our life, we honor our body with proper care to ensure that our new structure is physically and emotionally sound. To do this, we eliminate self-destructive behavior. We affirm ourselves for who we are. We recognize the gifts and graces that are ours to offer in service to God and others.

◦ Reconstruction is the work of faith.

- When we rebuild we build on the Rock—we partner with God. Faith inspires us to do the hard work of grief, the hand-work of reconstruction. "Unless the Lord builds the house, those who build it labor in vain" (Psalm 127:1 NRSV).

Choose Life

*Now choose life, so that you and your children may live and that you
may love the LORD your God, listen to his voice, and hold fast to him.
For the LORD is your life.*

—*Deuteronomy 30:19-20 NIV*

One day, someday, we find ourselves unexpectedly at the end of grief,
wavering still between the past and the future. This is the moment
when we decide emphatically to choose life. We rejoin life in the fullness
for which God created us. We honor the steadfast love and faithfulness of
God when we resolve to live the rest of the life that is ours empowered by
our own extraordinary gifts of grief.

Because God endows us with the capacity to think and reason, choice
is part of our everyday existence and behavior. We choose because we are
alive. When we err, God allows us to experience our choices and even the
consequences of our own free will.

We make hundreds of mindless choices each day: what to wear,
what to do, where to go, whom to see. Many difficult choices seem imper-
ative after the death of our husband or wife, a time when we are most
vulnerable:

- Where should I live?
- Must I get a job and work?
- What must I do to survive alone?
- What must I do to live today?
- What must I decide now?
- What decisions can wait?

Choice suggests that there are options, things to decide between or among:

- We decide not to choose. Why must we choose anything? When our grief will not be moved, we live in a state of mental, emotional, and spiritual inertia. This choice is for life in an illusory time and space that no longer exists.

- We choose to do nothing. If our existence is defined only by death, this is life *in memoriam*, dedicated solely to the memory of our husband or wife. This meager life has little future; it is a choice for dying while we are still alive. This is not how our spouse would want us to live.

- We choose to wait and see. This is a wise choice until gradually life becomes less about pain and sorrow and more about hope for the future. When we are ready, we will experience the urge to get off the sidelines and reenter life as an active participant. We wait and see, we choose and try, and try again until we find a satisfying rhythm of choice.

I wrote in a memoir:

And then, there comes that unexpected moment when we can no longer elude an unmistakable cue for rejoining life in its fullness. This does not mean that the work of grief is complete—there is no finite end to grief. Is this impetus, then, an illusion, one easily destroyed by the habit of hopelessness? I hold back, reluctant to trust and embrace this life that is mine. Do I cherish continued existence as the inhabitant of an empty shell? No, life is not for living on the half-shell. In that conscious moment of feeling more self-confident and again present to oneself—changed, but returned after a long and precarious absence from the world—we respond to that irresistible urge: our emotional readiness to engage and venture forth again.

It is reaching out to encounter a stranger for even a moment, testing to see if there is still a heart within to validate the mechanics of a long-unused smile. It is a thirst to be refilled by the adventure of life, to rediscover vitality after a long and arduous journey. It is that moment when you feel like wearing your red shoes again.

‿ We choose to move forward. Frankl states, "Everything can be taken from a man or woman but one thing: the last of human freedoms to choose one's attitude in any given set of circumstances, to choose one's own way."[62] The spirit in which to live is a conscious choice. We are in charge of our own emotional destiny. We may choose to live either in chronic misery as the victim of unrelieved sadness turned inward, or in faith, trusting the promise that God has a plan for our future. When we choose to move forward, we plan. We make informed decisions about our estate, our health care, and final arrangements. But we are not required to make all of tomorrow's choices today.

‿ We choose a life of selfless service. "Choose this day whom you will serve . . . but as for me and my household, we will serve the LORD" (Joshua 24:15 NRSV). When the end of our journey through grief nears, it is our responsibility—indeed, our sacred duty of grief—to choose life in love and service to God and others.

We choose, we grow, we live, we love, we serve. "Now choose life. . . . For the LORD is your life" (Deuteronomy 30:19-20 NIV).

Gifts of Your Spirit—
A Lasting Legacy

Precious in the sight of the LORD is the death of his faithful ones.

—*Psalm 116:15 NRSV*

In his book, *Longing for Enough in a Culture of More,* the Reverend Paul Escamilla describes those whose lives are well-lived as "durable saints." He writes:

> Among the varied ways faithfulness has become the fabric of their lives, one quality has been identifiable again and again: . . . a certain adequacy of means that issues forth in abundance for others.

> At their passing, these durable saints have signed the air not so much with fanfare as grace. The ledgers of their lives are long in matters of generosity, self-giving, and trust; more measured in the realm of acquisition and possessions; and slimmest of all in regard to recognition and self-promotion. In other words, over a lifetime they seem . . . to have needed little and offered much.[63]

Gifts of our spirit are the lasting legacy we leave behind when we die. They are ours to invest in those we love while we yet live. Our personal

143

legacy is not one of material possession or wealth. No amount of money or property can substitute for gifts of our spirit. Our legacy reflects the spiritual maturity of our grief, survived and at last conquered. The Apostle Paul expressed this hope, "I pray also that the eyes of your heart may be enlightened in order that you may know the hope to which he has called you, the riches of his glorious inheritance in the saints, and his incomparably great power for us who believe" (Ephesians 1:18-19 NIV).

Our endowment to others expresses our personal gifts of our spirit. These are the eternal qualities of our life, the durable substance of spirit that lives on after we die. These qualities form our lasting legacy:

- *Love.* "And the greatest of these is love" (1 Corinthians 13:13 NRSV). If we could give but one gift, the greatest would be love. Leighton marked Colossians 3:14 in his New Testament: "And, above everything else, be truly loving, for love is the golden chain of all the virtues" (3:14 JBP). Consider how you see your love reflected in others. It is true that you are not responsible for whether or not the love you give is received. Perhaps you have known personally or experienced family dysfunction and estrangement. This is usually the result of human free-will choices and decisions. There are no perfect families. What you can do, however, is determine the way in which you express and give love, regardless of how it may be received. When you love without expectation, you are indeed a durable saint—needing little, offering much.

- *Goodness.* "Surely goodness and mercy shall follow me all the days of my life" (Psalm 23:6 NRSV). A life of authentic goodness inspires and enriches others by example. A pure heart and unmixed motives are manifestations of genuine goodness, the lasting legacy of a memorable life. This is how to build a life of authentic goodness: "His divine power has given us everything needed for life and godliness, through the knowledge of him who called us by his own glory and goodness...For this very reason, you must make every effort to support your faith with goodness, and goodness with knowledge, and knowledge with self-control, and self-control with endurance, and endurance with godliness, and godliness with mutual affection, and mutual affection with love" (2 Peter 1:3-7 NRSV). These are the steps, beginning with faith and ending with love. This is the biblical standard for authentic goodness.

Service. "Serve one another in love" (Galatians 5:13 NIV). A heart of service thrives in perpetuity. Imperceptibly we contribute to the formation of others as we model selfless servant leadership. When we "serve one another in love," we give the gift of ourselves. Joan Wester Anderson writes, "We can all be angels to one another. We can choose to obey the still small stirring within, the little whisper that says 'Go. Ask. Reach out. Be an answer to someone's plea. You have a part to play. Have faith.' We can decide to risk that He is indeed there, watching, caring, cherishing us as we love and accept love. The world will be a better place for it. And wherever they are, the angels will dance."[64]

Faith. We give the gift of faith and teach our faith by example. Those we love learn best about our faith by how we live. Our spiritual estate is character and integrity, formed by the discipline of faith. "I know, my God, that you test the heart and are pleased with integrity" (1 Chronicles 29:17 NIV). God tests our heart and is pleased with integrity, the measure of a life well-lived in faith.

Compassion. We are benefactors of compassion when we reach out with a heart fortified from within by our experience of grief. We best teach compassion to those we love by our spiritual reaction to life's trials and tragedies. Our gift of compassion to others is never forgotten. There is perhaps no finer gift of our spirit than to endow those we love with a sensibility for compassion.

It would be our worthiest epitaph if we live as durable saints and one day die to our glorious inheritance in the saints knowing that we have created a lasting legacy by giving the gifts of our eternal spirit to those we love.

Pain and sorrow are vanquished by faith, death rendered powerless as we at last traverse the valley of the shadow of death and grief is no more. Dr. Margaret A. Farley, Professor of Christian Ethics at Yale Divinity School writes, "Faith leads us, it is true, through valleys of darkness and into the shadow of death. But all the while, it leads into life, and it knows the ways not only of sadness, but of joy. By it we are carried into God's own life; in it we can find one another; through it we come home even to ourselves. Incredible work, radical surrender, unlimited future, inexhaustible life—these are not illusions only if it is true that 'Nothing is impossible with God.' If these are not illusions, then they do bear pondering, even as aspects of the concept of faith—believing, believing in and believing into the God who has been revealed in Jesus Christ."[65]

On the last occasion that my beloved husband was in the pulpit, he offered this pastoral prayer, a benediction to our grief journey, "We have come this far by faith, and we will continue to walk with our hand in yours wherever you lead us." Death has not left us ambivalent in our resolve to claim new life at the end of our journey through grief. Thanks be to God for the victory over death.

PART III

Beside the Broken Heart

Grief at the Holidays: The Season

I will be with you; I will not fail you or forsake you.

—Joshua 1:5 NRSV

The journey through grief is marked by inevitable secular and sacred holidays. Even under the best circumstances, holidays are usually emotion-laden. The nature of grief is that it intensifies our experience of those occasions that painfully remind us of our loss. With the rapid succession of Thanksgiving, Christmas, and the New Year, November and December can be painful, prolonged days of remembrance that are magnified by our grief. When we grieve at the holidays, we agonize about what is to come because of the unknown—how things will be rather than how things have been. As we live in the shadow of expectation we cherish both high hopes and dismal fears. Most often our reality is somewhere in between.

When print advertising and television commercials assault us prematurely with stealth campaigns that inevitably draw our attention to the extended holiday season, we may react with instinctive aversion. It seems that advertising and decorating begin earlier each year.

Many people dread the holidays because of the unavoidable pressure to do, buy, and experience all that is urged upon us during the season. Dread

149

may creep into our hearts as we begin to imagine what the holiday season will be like. We wonder, "How can there be celebration without the one I love?" It is normal to be fearful when we are grieving, especially as we anticipate or even dread the holiday season. Dread is "fearful or distasteful anticipation,"[66] which may express itself as disquiet, worry, or distress, some of the familiar emotions of grief. Dread is, in fact, the extreme form of fear.

> *Be strong and of good courage, do not fear or be in dread . . . for it is the* Lord *your God who goes with you; he will not fail you or forsake you.*
> —*Deuteronomy 31:6 RSV*

To best understand dread at the holidays, remember that fear is a basic human response, especially when we are grieving. As we approach the season, remember that *anticipation is usually much worse than the actual holiday*. Often we resolve much of our fear ahead of time and the day is not as difficult as we expected.

> *For I, the Lord your God, hold your right hand; it is I who say to you, "Do not fear, I will help you."*
> —*Isaiah 41:13 NRSV*

If this is the first holiday season without your husband or wife, you may be engulfed by a tidal wave of emotion. When we grieve at the holidays, our heart is attuned to the sadness of loss and pain. If you are tearful or depressed, your heartfelt tears may cue your family members to express their emotions as well. Worry about crying is a hardship of grief compounded by the holidays. When we release our tears, we experience physical and emotional relief, a welcome catharsis to our grief.

As you grieve at this affective time of the year, these coping strategies may help you through the holidays:

🕊 Put the day in perspective.

The actual holiday is just one day, twenty-four hours. For weeks on end, life is pressured by commercial, social, and spiritual suggestions that demand a larger-than-life experience of the holidays. Inflamed by the secular world, intense emotions overlay grief for what seems an interminable holiday season. The holiday itself is just one day. Put the day in perspective.

🕊 Know your limits.

Be intentional about the extent to which you participate—how little or how much you want to do. You are the only person in charge of you; be in touch with yourself. If a situation is too difficult, limit your exposure or choose not to take part. It is easy to be swept along by the good intentions of family and friends who want to distract you from your pain. If you are pressured to do too much, you may instinctively retreat. Know your limits; resolve not to exceed them. The word most seldom used at the holidays is "no." You may say "no"; do not be afraid to say "no." Just say "no."

🕊 Plan.

Before the death of your husband or wife, there was probably always a plan. If this is the first holiday without your spouse, make a plan and structure the holidays accordingly. Be timely in making airline/hotel reservations; communicate your plan to family. Whether your plan succeeds or is not quite what you expected, a plan for the holidays precludes the emotional hangover of discouragement and frustration if there is no plan at all. Make a plan. Have a plan.

↪ Take care of yourself.

- Get enough rest. The holidays are physically, emotionally, mentally, and spiritually draining.
- Consider having a "good enough" holiday, rather than a perfect holiday. Do not set expectations too high for yourself or the day. Before the death of your husband or wife, there were probably some disappointing holiday seasons.
- Think about how to make it through just this holiday. There will be other holidays.
- Live one day at a time; stay in the moment.
- Turn off the television and limit trips to retail environments.
- Do whatever you can to manage the daily, artificial urgency of the commercial holiday season.
- Guard your heart. The holidays are the most stressful time of the year. Grief causes real physical stress, which should not be trivialized or discounted. If you manifest any heart-related symptoms, seek immediate treatment.
- Take time for yourself on holidays—time to reflect, time to remember, time to forget.
- Let others know that they are not responsible for making you happy. Even if your husband or wife would "want you to be happy," you do not have to be happy. Being happy, however, is not a betrayal of your spouse. One day when life returns more to happiness, holidays will be easier to manage. The experience of most is that eventually they do enjoy the holidays again.

↪ Decide about traditions.

Holidays usually center on tradition. When life is fractured by death, you may decide to continue family traditions, or you may want to create new traditions that honor the memory of your husband or wife. What you do this year does not have to become a permanent tradition. Your experience of grief may change the way you approach the holidays; you may decide on a new format for the future.

❧ Be realistic about family.

At the holidays, you may want the "picture" to remain the same. That is, you would like to continue envisioning your family as it was before the death of your husband or wife. Many seasonal illustrations by Norman Rockwell idealize the family as a multi-generational group, clearly connected by warmth and love. You are perhaps convinced by these familiar images that family life should resemble the ideal. Contemporary experience affirms that art does not imitate life. Divorce, blended families, dysfunctional relationships, addictions, and ordinary bad behavior are the realities that belie the ideal of an intact nuclear family gathered together in peace to share a loving, joyful holiday celebration.

Though holidays mean "family together," gatherings may be difficult. Your family may want everything "back to normal." You may experience subtle pressure to be appropriately cheerful and gay; you may be expected to "be over it." Grief makes it difficult to participate fully in festivities. It seems that your family is trying to forget what you most want to remember.

Acting as if no one died denies grief at the very moment when the comfort of family is most needed. Be proactive and decide together about the holidays. Communicate and be sensitive to one other. Remember that there is no right or wrong way to experience the holidays, the season, or the actual twenty-four-hour day.

🕊 Realize that it is not going to be easy.

🕊 Do the things that are special or important to you.

🕊 Do the best that you can.

God knows your heart as you grieve at the holidays. Receive God's promise, "I will be with you; I will not fail you or forsake you" (Joshua 1:5 NRSV).

Grief at the Holidays: The Experience

To you is born this day in the city of David a Savior, who is the Messiah, the Lord.

—Luke 2:11 NRSV

Christmas may evoke memories that trigger and sustain our grief. The contrast between sorrow and celebration is almost unbearable because many of our best memories are perhaps in the context of holiday celebrations. We are painfully aware of the absence of our husband or wife, who was likely the most important person in our interpersonal sphere. Poet Edna St. Vincent Millay wrote, "The presence of that absence is everywhere."[67] We endow Christmas with emotional power as we remember the past with intense yearning for the one whose presence brought joy to our life.

We celebrate Christmas in two ways:

- the festival of Christmas
- the experience of Christmas

The festival of Christmas celebrates the day; our secular reference is tradition, skewed by grief. As we gather with family, or others we choose as family, we know that the festival of Christmas will never be the same again without our husband or wife.

155

- Is it too much effort to put up a tree?
- Do you decorate, or should the ornaments stay packed away this year?
- Is it too painful to send Christmas cards?
- Is gift selection a daunting task without the concurrence of your husband or wife?

Within the festival our heart seeks the deeper experience of Christmas. Sometimes it happens; sometimes it does not. For a while, our joy in the world may seem a remembrance from a life passed away. But Christmas may come to us in small, private moments when our heart is strangely touched by joy. The experience of Christmas may surprise us with the mystery of comfort. Amid the chaos of grief, the moment of Christmas may take our breath away with its life-renewing peace.

Grief is an opportunity to discover anew the true meaning of Christmas—God's love for humankind. Christmas happens when our heart discerns divine love indwelling. This is the love that holds us close in grief. This is the love that restores us and makes us whole again. Emmanuel, God with us,

- to comfort us
- to redeem us
- to restore us
- to give us peace
- to hold us in the communion of saints with the one we have loved and lost

Look for a sign; it will overwhelm you as the certainty of life beyond death reaches into your heart with the unmistakable gift of God's love. The experience of Christmas may come to you any day, not just on

December 25. Expect it; look for it, be open to it. Christmas comes when someone reaches out to you in love. Christmas comes when you reach out to someone in love. Expect an unexpected blessing, be a blessing to others. Christmas. Emmanuel. God with us.

I am your friend and my love for you goes deep.
There is nothing I can give you which you have not got,
But there is much, very much,
That, while I cannot give it, you can take.
No Heaven can come to us
unless our hearts find rest in today.
Take Heaven!

No peace lies in the future
Which is not hidden in this present little instance.
Take Peace!

The gloom of the world is but a shadow.
Behind it, yet within our reach, is joy.

There is a radiance and glory in the darkness,
Could we but see—and to see we have only to look.
I beseech you to look!

Life is so generous a giver,
But we, judging its gifts by the covering,
Cast them away as ugly, or heavy or hard.
Remove the covering and you will find beneath it a living splendor,
Woven of love, by wisdom, with power.

Welcome it, grasp it,
And you touch the angel's hand that brings it to you.
Everything we call a trial, a sorrow, or a duty,
Believe me, that angel's hand is there,

The gift is there,
And the wonder of an overshadowing presence.
Our joys too, be not content with them as joys.
They too conceal diviner gifts.

Life is so full of meaning and purpose,
So full of beauty—beneath its covering—
That you will find earth but cloaks your heaven.

Courage, then, to claim it, that is all.
But courage you have,
And the knowledge that we are all pilgrims together,
Wending through unknown country, home.

And so, at this time, I greet you.
Not quite as the world sends greetings,
But with profound esteem and with the prayer that for you
Now and forever, the day breaks,
And the shadows flee away.

—Fra Giovanni Giocondo (1513)[68]

Grief at the Holidays: The Light

The people who walked in darkness have seen a great light; those who dwelt in the land of the shadow of death, upon them a light has shined.
—Isaiah 9:2 NKJV

Christmas lights symbolize the festival. Each one is a brilliant celebration of life. The reality of grief is that the death of our husband or wife has darkened our life. At Christmas, darkness seeks the light and becomes the light: "The people who walked in darkness have seen a great light; those who dwelt in the land of the shadow of death, upon them a light has shined" (Isaiah 9:2 NKJV). This is the light that shines out of our darkness, the promise that there is yet life beyond grief. Christmas is about the light of the world, God's love illuminating our darkness.

On a recent trip to New York, I landed at Newark Airport in New Jersey. From there, the most expeditious route into the city is through the Holland Tunnel under the Hudson River, which leads directly into lower Manhattan. I was rather unsettled by the necessity of travelling at subterranean depths because I was in New York on September 11, 2001, and could never forget the fear and desperation of that horrible day. When we drove down the gradual incline into the tunnel, I knew that there was no turning back.

As I focused on the rather nondescript, clinical-looking tiled walls, I thought of the infrastructure supporting this extraordinary feat of engineering. So much more than just those million bits of ceramic hold back the tremendous hydraulic power of water. I was reminded that the unseen framework of that remarkable man-made tunnel is an apt metaphor for God's unseen presence at work in our life. As we grieve, he is the invisible foundation that holds and supports us, unshakeable and never changing.

In the middle of the tunnel a light flashed on top of a slowing maintenance truck a short distance ahead. My mind automatically raced through several worst case scenarios. Traffic slowed and then gradually stopped. The driver of the truck hopped out and quickly changed places with a colleague at the mid-way monitoring station. Apparently, it was lunch time. The entire exchange took perhaps five seconds. We gradually moved forward again and slowly ascended as light slowly bathed the end of the tunnel in the golden warmth of hope.

Light had been there all along—over, above, and outside the tunnel— unseen for the moments of travel from a suburb into a city, moments spent in a place of relative darkness submerged under a body of water. And so it is on our journey through grief. We descend for a while with no turning back as we enter a dark place. There are obstacles and stops along the way, yet we trust God, the infrastructure, to keep us safe. As we emerge from the tunnel of grief, darkness is at last overcome by the light of renewed life. It is the light of God's eternal love which guides our way through the dark passage that is grief, "for we walk by faith, not by sight" (2 Corinthians 5:7 NRSV).

The words of "Hymn for Advent" by John Ness Beck are powerful and evocative, "God says: Light! and makes our day; fear and chaos lose their say."[69] At Christmas, chaos all around us may roil our emotions. There may be chaos in our family or home. The clamor of the secular world may incite chaos in our heart. But chaos is overwhelmed and defeated by light.

Light is the reason for Christmas, the light of God's love, Emmanuel, God with us.

There are many incarnations of light—candlelight, incandescent light, sunlight, moonlight, the radiant brilliance of stars. The psalmist declares, "In your light we see light" (Psalm 36:9b NRSV). In grief, light is in the delicate balance between our sadness and our hope for the future. Light is in our heightened peace as we move toward acceptance. Light is in our enjoyment of one or two aspects of the holiday season, and in surviving largely intact. Light is in our understanding of the gift—joy. Indeed, "Light dawns for the righteous, and joy for the upright in heart" (Psalm 97:11 NRSV).

Our journey through grief is nuanced by contrasts of light and dark, which create shadow. We recognize this is as the long shadow cast by death. But within shadow is the suggestion of light. Without light there can be no shadow. In art, chiaroscuro is the distribution of light and shade. It is the use of deep variations and subtle gradations for dramatic effect, as in the paintings of Rembrandt. We make our way through the valley of the shadow of death because of light hidden within the shadow. At the end of our journey there is the promise of radiance.

We have the power to direct our grief as we direct the light. When we block the light and, instead, choose darkness, we become a holiday victim, for in darkness there is no light. Finding the light means managing the darkness. Unlike gradations of light, dark is dark; darkness is darkness. "If then the light in you is darkness, how great is that darkness!" (Matthew 6:23b NRSV). If you dwell in darkness, overwhelmed by negative emotions and immobilized by grief, ask for help. Let another guide you back into the light.

Grief may seem like an eternal night, as if our light is eclipsed for a while by darkness. Slowly, with divine radiance, receding darkness yields to dawn. The rosy aura of sunrise bathes the softness of morning with the light of reawakening life. As love and hope creep imperceptibly onto the horizon, we greet the new day of the rest of our life with expectation and tentative joy—our soul again enlivened by the warmth of light. See the light.

Just as there is no one experience of loss, there is no one experience of light. Light shines in quiet meditation. Light shines in moments of prayer and thanksgiving. It shines when we light a candle to honor the memory of our spouse. Our shared light shines forever. Love is the divine link to the eternal spiritual presence of the one you have loved and lost. As you create light and discover your light within, each day holds the promise of remembrance, release, and expression. Walk in the light.

Christmas is the celebration of light. Light alone guides our way through the dark passage of grief. Receive the blessing when moments of light shine in your heart. Be at peace in the certainty that death is not the end. Seek the light.

Preparing for Death

We brought absolutely nothing with us when we entered the world and we can be sure we shall take absolutely nothing with us when we leave it.

—*1 Timothy 6:7-8 JBP*

On a beach vacation in January, 2004, I sat on a beautiful chaise one afternoon, reading a book as warm sunlight streamed into the room. The steady cadence of ocean waves accompanied the rhythm of a soft tropical breeze. I was at peace; life in that moment was carefree and full of contentment. My beloved husband, Leighton, sat in the next room, resting and relaxing. Our life together seemed perfect, complete in every way—not because we were on holiday, but because we were married and had each other to love and cherish. Three months later Leighton was diagnosed with pancreatic cancer, an overwhelmingly terminal disease. Ninety days later he was dead. This is life. This is death. This is how life unravels when we least expect it.

"We brought absolutely nothing with us when we entered the world and we can be sure we shall take absolutely nothing with us when we leave it" (1 Timothy 6:7-8 JBP). This bold, infinitely true admonition is a powerful reminder of our mortality. The fact of life and death is that we came into the world with nothing except our body and soul. We leave with nothing but our soul.

Death is an inescapable part of life. We prepare with great intention for most of life; much of our time is spent "getting ready to begin." We prepare for personal and social participation in the world each day. We prepare for work. We prepare for retirement. Yet we are reluctant to prepare for death, the one inevitable experience shared by all.

❦ Is it too painful to think about dying?

❦ Are we afraid to contemplate the end of life?

❦ Is death simply inconceivable?

We are not in control of death. "For everything there is a season, and a time for every matter under heaven: a time to be born, and a time to die" (Ecclesiastes 3:1-2 NRSV). What we can control is planning for death—that is, preparing in advance on our own behalf. When we take action in life, we prepare for death. As we take charge, we answer our own lingering question, "Who is going to do the business of planning for me?" We are blessed with peace of mind when we direct our own end of life. Preparation eases our death for our children, family, and friends. It is a priceless gift to those we love.

The death of our husband or wife necessitates the modification of our estate documents. Likely your spouse was named executor, heir, or beneficiary of your estate. Because of the changes triggered by death, we must now entrust our private information to a third party other than our spouse, to someone who will execute our directives at death. A child, advisor, or friend you trust implicitly needs to know and understand the details of your life, your business, and your specific preferences at death.

You will have new insight into your estate as you share information with your executor.

 Be certain that you have these essential documents, updated and fully executed:

- Last Will and Testament
- Statutory Durable Power of Attorney
- Durable Power of Attorney for Health Care
- Directive to Physicians/Living Will (must be HIPAA* compliant)
- HIPAA* Authorization
- Organ Donor Directive

*(Health Insurance Portability and Accountability Act of 1996, HIPAA, Title II)

If you do not have these basic documents, consult your attorney or estate planner about preparing the legal instruments necessary to facilitate your care and well-being in life and the execution of your directives at death.

Be certain that you and others know where these documents are located:

- Birth certificates/Adoption papers
- Marriage License
- Trust documents
- Safe Deposit box keys
- Other important keys
- Check books/Savings books
- Installment Loan payment books (mortgage, car, etc.)
- Employment income records
- Bank statements/Cancelled checks

❧ Brokerage/Investment statements

❧ Retirement Plan (IRA, etc.) statements

❧ Computer programs/ Online Account information

Insurance Policies:

❧ Long-term Care

❧ Accident/Disability

❧ Health

❧ Life

❧ Property

❧ Automobile

❧ Liability

Real Estate Documents:

❧ Title/Deed to home

❧ Title/Deed to other Real Property

❧ Mortgage documents

❧ Property records (leases, liens, etc.)

❧ Warranties/Guarantees

If you store signed original documents in a safe deposit box, make sure that copies, along with your directives, are readily available. Easy access can spare family and executors the frustration of not knowing the "where, when, what, how, and why" of your life.

The death of our husband or wife causes us to consider our own final arrangements. Taking the necessary steps to plan your funeral is an expression of care and concern for those you leave behind. From first-hand experience, you know what to do at the time of death; you should assume that others do not. Confusion, inefficiency, delays, and heartache are minimized when family and executors are familiar with your final wishes and directives before you die.

After the initial legalities have been satisfied, your funeral plans and arrangements should be carried out according to your specified wishes. When you stipulate your plans in detail in writing, you eliminate the need for many critical decisions, relieving your family of this burden when you die. It is difficult to make wise, discerning decisions at a time of urgency. Death strains the emotions of most families and sometimes ignites disputes.

If you have not prepared, there are over fifty decisions that will have to be made within a very short time after death:

- Gifts of my body
- Death certificate information
- Obituary notice
- Funeral/memorial service
- Alternative service options
- Disposition of body
- Cemetery lot/entombment
- Personal appearance
- Viewing/visitation
- Grave marker
- Memorial gifts
- People to notify

Consider pre-paying or providing financial resources (designated bank account, life insurance policy, burial policy, etc.) for your final arrangements. The amount should be adequate and readily available for this purpose. The funeral provider you select will identify the costs. If you do not make provision for payment, a funeral can be financially devastating for your family. You comfort others in death when you do not leave this expense for someone else to pay.

Grief is incomprehensible until it is experienced. If our experience of loss and survival eases the suffering of those we love when we die, we reach out to them from eternity to extend the hard-won gifts of our own grief. When we prepare for death we allow those we love a glimpse into our soul, the one thing with which we depart this earth when we die. "We brought absolutely nothing with us when we entered the world and we can be sure we shall take absolutely nothing with us when we leave it" (1Timothy 6:7-8 JBP). Prepare. Be at peace.

Peace of Mind— Financial Management for Life

For God has not given us a spirit of fear, but of power and of love and of a sound mind.

—2 Timothy 1:7 NKJV

Financial management can be a daunting challenge for anyone at any time of life. It is especially important with advancing age, in the event of illness, or at death. Personal business and financial management can easily overwhelm us, especially when we grieve.

After Leighton's death, I spent several months struggling to make order out of our personal business. Because of my experience with financial management through grief, I prepared the information in this chapter to assist others with the management of their business after the death of a loved one. You may feel barely adequate to the task of financial management, but there is no standard; where you are is good enough. *Not knowing* causes fear, which is part of every crisis in life. The information provided here is very basic. It is not about creating or amassing wealth. It is about empowering you to successfully manage what you have. The desired goals are as follows:

1. RELIEF FROM CHAOS through simplified financial understanding and management.
2. REASSURANCE and ENCOURAGEMENT that finances can be managed and mastered by anyone.
3. PEACE in the continuity of life, especially during advancing age, illness, and grief.

The fact is that *no one cares about your money like you care about your money*. Trusted advisors, children, and those who provide financial services may offer well-meant advice and recommendations, yet they are not personally invested in your financial health and well-being. When possible, no one should rely entirely on others for important financial management decisions unless he or she is physically or mentally unable to function or cope.

Our emotions about finances and money may be influenced by several factors:

- money attitudes learned from others
  - how our parents communicated about money
  - how we communicated with our spouse about money
  - our own self-confidence in personal money management

- our actual financial condition
  - our realistic understanding of our assets and liabilities
  - our commitment to living within our means

Managing money positively and proactively may benefit our changed life:

☙ empowerment—control over that which is quantifiable (money)

☙ peace of mind—learning hands-on management (finance and business)
   • understanding of what resources are available (income)
   • administration of day-to-day personal business (budgeting)

☙ financial independence

Money management is business. It does not merit an investment of the precious emotional energy that must be directed to issues of our heart, mind, and spirit when we grieve. Though you may feel inadequate to the task of your own financial management, remember that *no one cares about your money like you care about your money.* The following information is a guide for the preparation of a comprehensive, permanent record of personal and business information for your own reference and for those who assist you or will settle your estate. The discipline of financial management enables us to meet both opportunity and adversity with peace of mind.

There are four essential steps for effective financial management:

1. ASSESSMENT
2. ORGANIZATION
3. INVENTORY
4. ANALYSIS

As you move through these steps, there are five basic objectives:

1. Simplify.
2. Create a permanent record.
3. Develop a system of organization.

4. Create an accurate and comprehensive financial inventory.
5. Create a workable budget.

The information you will be assembling is a work in progress. Schedule an appointment with yourself and/or your advisors to review and update your information at least once a year. The goal is to create a workable system of financial management for your life going forward.

STEP 1: ASSESSMENT

Start now; start where you are; start with what you have. Begin with everyday tasks.

- Assemble the checkbooks. Determine how much money is available in the accounts on which you are authorized to sign. Could some accounts be closed or consolidated? Objectively assess your need for multiple bank accounts.
- Assemble the bills that must be paid. Pay these on time. Consider setting up automatic payments from a checking account for utility bills, mortgage payments, car payments, and monthly insurance premiums.
- Arrange for direct deposit of social security, pension, and paychecks into a designated account, which eliminates trips to the bank for deposit.
- Assemble files that are familiar and readily accessible.
- Make a general list—a preliminary overview—of your assets as you understand them.

The objective of ASSESSMENT is to take care of your business that requires immediate attention and generate a preliminary overview of your personal finances.

STEP 2: ORGANIZATION

Begin to assemble as much specific information as possible for your permanent record.

꙳ Devise a filing system that is logical and workable for you. What is efficient for one person may be difficult, inconvenient, or complicated for another.
  * Have a shredder to dispose of personal information, records, and files that are out of date or no longer needed.
  * Develop the habit of shredding mail (junk, solicitations, etc.) for protection against identity theft and fraud.
  * Register your telephone numbers with do-not-call lists as an additional privacy safeguard.

If the person who has been responsible for earning, providing, and managing is incapacitated or dies, take legal and emotional ownership of your assets.

The objective of ORGANIZATION is to create order and build a system for efficient financial management.

STEP 3: INVENTORY

Begin to make an inventory of your assets and liabilities.

꙳ Assemble information:
  * Real Estate/Real Property
  * Property Insurance
  * Credit Card Accounts

꙳ Using the forms on pages 175–183, prepare a statement of your:
  * Assets

- Liabilities
- Income

The objective of INVENTORY is to create a comprehensive, detailed record of your assets and liabilities.

STEP 4: ANALYSIS

Complete a comprehensive financial assessment using the forms on pages 175–183. Use the assembled information for:

✒ Your Personal Financial Inventory
✒ Your Personal Monthly Management Budget

The objective of ANALYSIS is for you to understand your assets and liabilities. This provides a clear picture of the standard of living you can reasonably expect and comfortably afford.

———————

Ongoing financial management—using the steps of ASSESSMENT, ORGANIZATION, INVENTORY, and ANALYSIS—is peace of mind that builds for the future. Your stewardship will honor your husband or wife for generations to come.

The forms and worksheets on the following pages are provided to help you create an overview of your personal business. These pages can be copied and used to begin and later update your management system as changes occur.

OVERVIEW OF ASSETS, LIABILITIES, INCOME
ASSETS

1. BANK ACCOUNTS

NAME OF ACCOUNT HOLDER(S) _____

NAME OF INSTITUTION _____

ACCOUNT NUMBER/STYLE   SIGNATORIES

CHECKING _____

APPROXIMATE BALANCE _____

MONEY MARKET SAVINGS _____

APPROXIMATE BALANCE _____

CERTIFICATE OF DEPOSIT _____

FACE VALUE _____

INTEREST RATE _____

MATURITY DATE _____

INTEREST _____

2. BROKERAGE ACCOUNTS

NAME OF ACCOUNT HOLDER _____

NAME OF INSTITUTION _____

SECURITIES HELD   SHARES   APPROXIMATE VALUE

STOCKS _____

_____

_____

BONDS _____

_____

_____

MUTUAL FUNDS _____

_____

_____

MONEY MARKET ACCOUNT(S) _____

_____

_____

3. MUTUAL FUND/INDIVIDUAL STOCK ACCOUNTS

NAME OF FUND/STOCK _____

NUMBER OF SHARES HELD/FUND BALANCE _____

NAME OF ACCOUNT HOLDER _____

PARTICIPANT NUMBER _____

NAME OF INSTITUTION _____

LIABILITIES

MORTGAGE LOANS:
    HOMESTEAD $

    SECOND HOME $

    RENTAL PROPERTIES $

    HOME EQUITY LOAN $

AUTOMOBILE LOANS/LEASES $

CREDIT CARD DEBT $

NOTES PAYABLE $

LOANS FROM BROKERAGE MARGIN ACCOUNT $

BANK LOANS $

UNPAID/DEFERRED IRS TAX LIABILITY $

ESTIMATE OF TOTAL LIABILITIES $_____

NET WORTH = ASSETS MINUS LIABILITIES $_____

ESTIMATE OF NET WORTH $_____

INCOME

SALARY AND BONUSES	$
DEFERRED COMPENSATION	$
SOCIAL SECURITY	$
PENSION PLAN	$
INVESTMENT INCOME	$
IRA	$
ALIMONY	$
CHILD SUPPORT	$

ESTIMATE OF TOTAL INCOME PER YEAR $____

ESTIMATE OF INCOME TAXES OWED PER YEAR $____

ESTIMATE OF NET INCOME PER YEAR $____

ESTIMATE OF TOTAL INCOME PER MONTH $____

PERSONAL FINANCIAL INVENTORY
ASSETS

CHECKING ACCOUNT(S)	$
SAVINGS ACCOUNT(S)	$
CERTIFICATES OF DEPOSIT	$
MONEY MARKET FUNDS	$

INVESTMENTS:

STOCKS	$
BONDS	$
MUTUAL FUNDS	$
IRA	$
ANNUITIES	$
LIFE INSURANCE AND DEATH BENEFITS	$

COMPANY BENEFITS:

STOCK OPTIONS	$
SAVINGS/401(k) PLANS	$
ESOP/PAYSOP	$
PENSION PLAN	$
DEFERRED COMPENSATION	$

REAL ESTATE:

HOMESTEAD	$
SECOND HOME	$
RENTAL PROPERTIES	$
MORTGAGES/DEEDS RECEIVABLE	$
REAL PROPERTY:	
OIL AND GAS INTERESTS	$
PARTNERSHIP INTERESTS	$

PERSONAL PROPERTY:
    FINE ART $
    JEWELRY $
    HOUSEHOLD FURNISHINGS $
    AUTOMOBILES $
    OTHER PERSONAL EFFECTS $

ESTIMATE OF TOTAL ASSETS $_____

PERSONAL MONTHLY MANAGEMENT BUDGET

GROSS INCOME:

SALARY/WAGES/COMPENSATION $

SOCIAL SECURITY $

IRA $

ANNUITY $

PENSION PLAN $

INVESTMENT INCOME $

<u>**ESTIMATE OF TOTAL GROSS MONTHLY INCOME**</u> $____

<u>**ESTIMATE OF TOTAL GROSS ANNUAL INCOME**</u> $____

PERSONAL MONTHLY MANAGEMENT BUDGET

EXPENSES:

HOUSING:
    RENT/MORTGAGE $
    ASSOCIATION FEES OR DUES $
    INSURANCE $
    TAXES $
    HOME MAINTENANCE $

UTILITIES:
    GAS $
    ELECTRICITY $
    WATER $
    TELEPHONE $
    CABLE/INTERNET SERVICE $
    CREDIT CARD/INSTALLMENT DEBT $
    STUDENT/EDUCATION LOANS $

TRANSPORTATION:
    AUTOMOBILE LOAN/LEASE PAYMENT $
    GAS/MAINTENANCE $
    INSURANCE $

FOOD $
MEDICAL $
WORK-RELATED EXPENSES $
PENSION/401(k) CONTRIBUTION $
IRA CONTRIBUTION $

SAVINGS $

SUPPORT OF DEPENDENT(S) $

TAXES:
   PROPERTY TAXES $
   INCOME TAXES $

CHARITABLE CONTRIBUTIONS $

INSURANCE:
   LIFE INSURANCE $
   HEALTH INSURANCE $
   LONG-TERM CARE INSURANCE $
   UMBRELLA LIABILITY INSURANCE $

PROPERTY INSURANCE:
   SCHEDULED PROPERTY $
   JEWELRY $

PERSONAL EXPENSES:
   CLOTHING $
   ENTERTAINMENT $
   TRAVEL $
   EDUCATION $
   GIFTS $
   PERSONAL ITEMS $

ESTIMATE OF TOTAL MONTHLY EXPENSES $_____
ESTIMATE OF TOTAL ANNUAL EXPENSES $_____

ACTION PLAN

This ACTION PLAN is a reminder of the information it is important to have available at any time, especially at the time of death.

1. Review your personal documents and revise as needed.
   - Statutory Durable Power of Attorney
   - Medical Power of Attorney
   - Living Will/Directives to Physicians
   - Last Will and Testament
   - Trust Agreements
   - Burial Arrangements/Funeral Plans/Obituary Notice

2. Contact the Social Security Administration.
   - Report the death.
   - Request the necessary changes for survivor benefit payments.
   - Apply for one-time death benefit ($255.00).
   - Request direct deposit of social security benefit to designated checking account.

3. Work with your CPA and attorney to file:
   - Estate Tax Return—due 9 months after date of death
   - Federal and State Tax Returns

4. Other contacts:
   - Insurance Companies
     - Request claim forms.
     - File for benefits.
     - Request form 712 (paid insurance claims) for Estate Tax Return.

- Banks/Credit Unions
  - Report the death.
  - Check for insurance coverage on loans.
- Current and Former Employers
  - Report the death.
  - Check for potential benefits - group insurance, pension, etc.
- Professional, fraternal, other associations
  - Report the death.
  - Cancel publications.
  - Request refund of unused dues.
  - Check for assistance or benefits.
- Department of Veterans Affairs in the case of military service.

5. Review your life insurance, property insurance, auto insurance, and liability insurance.
   - Ensure that the ownership of the policy is correct and current.
   - Ensure that the beneficiary designations are current.

6. Consult with a tax professional before making decisions regarding:
   - Joint accounts
   - Titles and deeds to vehicles and/or real estate
   - Retirement and investment accounts

Note: Ownership changes and asset transfers may have tax implications, best evaluated by a tax professional or attorney.

7. Credit cards
   - Payoff and/or cancel individual store credit cards; use one or two major credit cards for any non-cash purchases.
   - Consolidate multiple card accounts (more than one American Express, MasterCard, Visa) into one card per provider.

❧ Change the cardholder name on credit card accounts to you as primary/sole card holder.

❧ Inquire about possible life insurance or accidental death insurance benefits payable through the credit card company.

8. Obtain a copy of your credit report from one of the major credit reporting companies (Equifax, Experian, Transunion).

 ❧ Notify the credit reporting companies of a death. Ensure that the social security number is not being used fraudulently.

 ❧ Consider a credit watch service (approximate cost $100 per year). Immediate notification is provided if there are irregularities on credit accounts or unusual activity using your name or social security number.

9. Use the "belt and suspenders" approach to matters of personal safety.

 ❧ Do you have a home fire extinguisher?

   • Where is it?

   • How old is it?

   • Do you know how to use it?

   • Multi-purpose extinguishers are available in a variety of sizes. Ensure that one is accessible and you know how to activate it. For peace of mind you may want to have a fire extinguisher in the kitchen, the laundry room/area, the garage, and/or your bedroom.

 ❧ Does your house have a smoke detector/alarm?

   • Is it battery-powered?

   • Do you have a regular schedule for changing the batteries?

 ❧ Does your house have a carbon monoxide detector/alarm?

   • Do you need to consider having one installed?

 ❧ Do you have a 24-hour pharmacy?

- Do you know the telephone number?
- Is delivery service available?
- Is there a drive-through window for pick-up?
- Are you registered at the pharmacy if a physician needs to call in a prescription during the night?

Do you have a medical condition for which you should wear a medic alert bracelet?

If you live alone, should you consider having a personal in-home monitoring system?

If you drive an older car, do you have an extended warranty?

- Is a roadside assistance service readily available through AAA, an extended warranty plan, automobile dealership, or satellite tracking service such as Onstar?
- Do you have a cellular phone in the car in the event of an emergency or need? Is it charged? Do you know how to use it to get help if needed?

Do you have a service warranty for the appliances in your home?

- A service warranty (not the same as the manufacturer's warranty for new appliances) covers service calls and repairs to most major appliances. Repairs can be expensive, unanticipated, unbudgeted costs.

Notes

1. *The Plays and Sonnets of William Shakespeare*, Volume One (Chicago: Encyclopaedia Britannica, Inc., 1952), 515.

2. Henry Scott Holland, Canon of St. Paul's Cathedral, from a sermon, "The King of Terrors," delivered in St. Paul's Cathedral on May 15, 1910, while the body of King Edward VII was lying in state at Westminster. http://en.wikisource.org/wiki/The_King_of_Terrors, accessed August 9, 2011.

3. Thomas Merton, *Thoughts in Solitude* (New York: Farrar, Straus and Giroux, 1999), 79.

4. S. Austin Allibone, *Prose Quotations from Socrates to Macaulay* (Philadelphia: J.P. Lippincott & Co., 1880), 37.

5. Harold Kushner, *When Bad Things Happen to Good People* (New York: Anchor Books, 1982), 140.

6. C. S. Lewis, *A Grief Observed* (San Francisco: HarperCollins, 1961), 3.

7. *The American Heritage Dictionary of the English Language*, Fourth Edition (Boston: Houghton Mifflin Company, 2006).

8. Edmund Burke, *A Philosophical Inquiry into the Origin of Our Ideas of the Sublime and Beautiful* (New York: Oxford University Press, Inc. 2008), 53.

9. Dag Hammarskjöld, *Markings* (New York: Random House, Inc., 2006), 85.

10. Elisabeth Kübler-Ross, M. D., *On Death and Dying* (New York: Touchstone, 1997).

11. Leighton K. Farrell, *Cries from the Cross* (Nashville: Abingdon Press, 1994), 46–47.

12. *Roget's II: The New Thesaurus*, Third Edition (Boston: Houghton Mifflin Harcourt Publishing Company, 2003).

13. Hans Küng, *On Being a Christian*, (Garden City: Doubleday & Company, Inc., 1976), 436.

14. *The American Heritage Dictionary of the English Language,* Fourth Edition (Boston: Houghton Mifflin Company, 2006).

15. Doug Manning, *Don't Take My Grief Away from Me* (Oklahoma City: In-Sight Books, 2003), 91.

16. Leighton K. Farrell, "Grief and Death," sermon preached at Highland Park United Methodist Church, Dallas, TX, February 12, 1995.

17. *Online Etymology Dictionary.* Douglas Harper, Historian. http://www.etymonline.com.

18. Hans Selye, "A Syndrome produced by Diverse Nocuous Agents," *Nature* 138 (1936): 32–34.

19. Thomas H. Holmes and Richard H. Rahe, "The Social Readjustment Rating Scale," *Journal of Psychosomatic Research* Vol. 11 (2), Aug. 1967: 213–18.

20. Sidney Cobb, M.D., "Presidential Address, 1976," *Psychosomatic Medicine* Vol. 38(5), Sep.–Oct. 1976: 300–314.

21. Henri Nouwen, *Sabbatical Journey: The Diary of His Final Year* (New York: The Crossroad Publishing Company, 1998), 220.

22. James Allen, *The Life Triumphant: Mastering the Heart and Mind* (Blacksburg: Wilder Publications, LLC, 2009), 8.

23. Viktor E. Frankl, *Man's Search for Meaning* (Boston: Beacon Press, 2006), 112–13.

24. Ibid., 146.

25. Molly Fumia, *Safe Passage* (York Beach, ME: Conari Press, 2003), 205.

26. George Eliot, *Adam Bede* (Oxford: Oxford University Press, 2008), 435–36.

27. *Roget's II: The New Thesaurus,* Third Edition (Boston: Houston Mifflin Harcourt Publishing Company, 2003).

28. Patsy Brundige and Pat Millican, *Hope for a Widow's Shattered World* (Lincoln: iUniverse, 2005), 61.

29. Mitch Albom, "If You Had One Day With Someone Who's Gone...," *Parade,* September 17, 2006.

30. Percy Bysshe Shelley, *To a Skylark, The Oxford Book of English Verse: 1250–1900* (Oxford: Clarendon, 1919), 608.

31. William Barclay, *The Gospel of John: The New Daily Study Bible* (Louisville: Westminster / John Knox Press 2001), 46.

32. Robert McAfee Brown, as quoted in Molly Fumia, *Safe Passage* (York Beach, ME: Conari Press, 2003), 245.

33. Elizabeth Barrett Browning, *Sonnets from the Portuguese and Other Love Poems* (Garden City: Doubleday & Company, Inc., 1954), 57.

34. Leighton K. Farrell, "The Will of God," sermon preached at Highland Park United Methodist Church, Dallas, TX, September 30, 1984.

35. Jan Richardson, *In Wisdom's Path* (Cleveland: Pilgrim Press, 2000), 124.

36. Leighton K. Farrell, "Grief and Death," sermon preached at Highland Park United Methodist Church, Dallas, TX, February 12, 1995.

37. Horatius Bonar, *Hymns of Faith and Hope* (London: James Nesbit, 1861), 52–54.

38. H. Henry Taylor, *Philip Van Artevelde* (1834), part 1, act 1, scene 5.

39. See "As 9/11 Draws Near, a Debate Rises: How Much Tribute Is Enough?" by N. R. Kleinfield, *New York Times*, September 2, 2007, http://www.nytimes.com/2007/09/02/nyregion/02fatigue.html.

40. John Ness Beck, "The Quiet Heart" (Columbus, OH: Beckenhorst Press, Inc., 1981).

41. Henri Nouwen, *Turn My Mourning into Dancing* (Nashville: Thomas Nelson, 2001), 76.

42. Eda LeShan quotation, http://www.quoteworld.org/quotes/8214, accessed August 9, 2011.

43. Paul Tillich, *The Eternal Now* (New York: Charles Scribner's Sons, 1963), 17–18, 21.

44. William Penn, in a 1699 tract written to his children as he prepared for a voyage, quoted in *The Friends' Library*, vol. 5, William Evans and Thomas Evans, eds. (Philadelphia: The Religious Society of Friends, 1841), 299.

45. William Barclay, *The Gospel of John: The New Daily Study Bible* (Louisville: Westminster John Knox Press, 2001), 1.

46. Henry L. Carrigan, Jr., Editor, *The Temple: The Poetry of George Herbert* (Brewster, MA: Paraclete Press, 2001), 8.

47. Henri Nouwen, *Turn My Mourning into Dancing* (Nashville: Thomas Nelson, 2001), 80.

48. Marcus Aurelius quotation, 1-Famous-Quotes.com, Gledhill Enterprises, 2011.http://www.1-famous-quotes.com/quote/547808, accessed August 9, 2011.

49. John M. Tyler, *The Whence and the Whither of Man: A Brief History of His Origin and Development Through Conformity to Environment; being the Morse lectures of 1895* (New York: Charles Scribner's Sons, 1899), 212.

50. Eric Hoffer, *The Ordeal of Change* (New York: Harper & Row, 1963), 1.

51. Henri J.M. Nouwen, *The Inner Voice of Love: A Journey Through Anguish to Freedom* (New York: Doubleday, 1998), 34–35.

52. Elisabeth Sifton, *The Serenity Prayer: Faith and Politics in Times of Peace and War* (New York: W.W. Norton & Company, Inc., 2005), 277.

53. Ashley Davis Prend, *Transcending Loss* (New York: Berkley Publishing Group, 1997), xvi.

54. Molly Fumia, *Safe Passage* (York Beach, ME: Conari Press, 2003), 98.

55. *The American Heritage Dictionary of the English Language*, Fourth Edition (Boston: Houghton Mifflin Company, 2006).

56. Elizabeth Gilbert, *Eat, Pray, Love* (New York: Viking Penguin Group, 2006), 260.

57. Joseph Addison, http://thinkexist.com/quotation/three_grand_essentials_to_happiness_in_this_life/148198.html.

58. David F. Allen, *In Search of the Heart* (McLean, VA: Curtain Call Productions, 2004), 174.

59. Molly Fumia, *Safe Passage* (York Beach, ME: Conari Press, 2003), 114.

60. Thesaurus.com. *Roget's 21st Century Thesaurus*, Third Edition (Philip Lief Group, 2009).

61. Oliver Goldsmith, *The Captivity, An Oratorio* (1764), Act II, Scene 1.

62. Viktor E. Frankl, *Man's Search for Meaning* (Boston: Beacon Press, 2006), 66.

63. Paul Escamilla, *Longing for Enough in a Culture of More* (Nashville: Abingdon Press, 2007), 4–5.

64. Joan Wester Anderson, *Where Angels Walk, True Stories of Heavenly Visitors* (Sea Cliff, NY: Barton & Brett Publishers, Inc., 1992), 233.

65. Margaret A. Farley, "Forms of Faith," *The Living Pulpit* 1:2 (April/June, 1992), 4–5.

66. *The American Heritage Dictionary of the English Language*, Fourth Edition (Boston: Houghton Mifflin Company, 2006).

67. Edna St. Vincent Millay, as quoted in Nancy Milford, *Savage Beauty: The Life of Edna St. Vincent Millay* (New York: Random House, 2002), 328.

68. Fra Giovanni Giocondo, from a letter written to Countess Allagia Aldobrandeschi on Christmas Eve, 1513.

69. Fred Kaan and John Ness Beck, *A Hymn for Advent* (Carol Stream, IL: Hope Publishing Company, 1975, 1977).

Also Available

A support and ministry program for those who are grieving

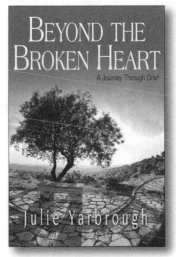